Transport, Regulation and Control

Mary Jones

Series editor
Fred Webber

CAMBRIDGE
UNIVERSITY PRESS

PUBLISHED BY THE PRESS SYNDICATE OF THE UNIVERSITY OF CAMBRIDGE
The Pitt Building, Trumpington Street, Cambridge CB2 1RP, United Kingdom

CAMBRIDGE UNIVERSITY PRESS
The Edinburgh Building, Cambridge CB2 2RU, United Kingdom
40 West 20th Street, New York, NY 10011-4211, USA
10 Stamford Road, Oakleigh, Melbourne 3166, Australia

© University of Cambridge Local Examinations Syndicate 1995

First published 1995
Fourth printing 1998

Printed in the United Kingdom at the University Press, Cambridge

A catalogue record for this book is available from the British Library

ISBN 0 521 42202 7 paperback

Designed and produced by Gecko Ltd, Bicester, Oxon

This book is one of a series produced to support
individual modules within the Cambridge Modular
Sciences scheme. Teachers should note that written
examinations will be set on the content of each module as
defined in the syllabus. This book is the author's
interpretation of the module.

Cover photograph: The Telegraph Colour Library

Contents

Acknowledgements

The author wishes to thank Mr W H Cousins for the data in table 2.1.

Photographs

1.4, 1.5, 1.12, 2.2, 2.4a, 3.8b, 3.13, 3.14, 4.4b, 6.2, 6.8, 6.9, 6.11, Biophoto Associates; 1.10a, Andrew Syred 1990 Microscopix Photolibrary; 1.10b, Andrew Syred 1991 Microscopix Photolibrary; 1.13b, 4.4a, Life Science Images; 2.10, Simon Fraser, Coronary Care Unit, Freeman Hospital, Newcastle/Science Photo Library; 3.2, Dr Jeremy Burgess/Science Photo Library; 3.8a, Andrew Syred 1994 Microscopix Photolibrary; 3.17, D. Brownell/The Image Bank; 4.13, Simon Fraser, Royal Victoria Infirmary, Newcastle/Science Photo Library.

The publishers would like to thank Michael Reiss and David Baylis for their help with the text.

Chapter one

The transport system of mammals

By the end of this chapter you should be able to:

1 explain why multicellular animals need transport mechanisms;

2 describe the structure of arteries, veins and capillaries, and relate their structure to their functions;

3 recognise micrographs of arteries, veins and capillaries;

4 describe the functions of tissue fluid, and its formation from blood plasma;

5 describe the functions of lymph, and its formation from tissue fluid;

6 describe the composition of blood;

7 outline the functions of white blood cells and platelets;

8 describe the role of haemoglobin in the transport of oxygen and carbon dioxide;

9 describe and explain the oxygen dissociation curve for haemoglobin;

10 describe and explain the effects of raised carbon dioxide concentrations on the haemoglobin dissociation curve (the Bohr effect);

11 describe and explain the differences between oxygen dissociation curves for haemoglobin, fetal haemoglobin and myoglobin, and explain the significance of these differences.

Why do humans have a blood system? The answer is fairly obvious even to a non-scientist: our blood system transports food and oxygen around the body. However, there are many organisms which have much less complex transport systems, and many which do not have any kind of transport system at all. Before looking in detail at the human transport system, it is worth briefly considering why some organisms can manage without one.

A quick survey of some organisms which have very simple transport systems, or even none at all, will provide an important clue. *Table 1.1* lists six kinds of organisms, and gives a brief summary of the type of transport system which they have.

SAQ 1.1

From *table 1.1*, state whether each of the following factors appears to be important in deciding whether or not an organism needs an efficient transport system. In each case, identify the information in the table which led you to your answer.

a Size **b** Level of activity

All living cells require a supply of nutrients, such as glucose. Most living cells also need a constant supply of oxygen. There will also be waste products, such as carbon dioxide, to be disposed of. Very small organisms, such as *Paramecium*, can meet their requirements for the supply of nutrients and oxygen, and the removal of waste products, by means of **diffusion.** The very small distances across which substances have to diffuse means that the speed of supply or removal is sufficient for their needs.

Even larger organisms, such as cnidarians, can manage by diffusion alone. Their body is made up of just two layers of cells, so every cell is within a very small distance of the water in which these organisms live and with which they exchange materials. Moreover, cnidarians are not very active animals, so their cells do not have large requirements for glucose or oxygen, nor do they produce large amounts of waste products. Diffusion, slow though it is, is quite adequate to supply their needs.

Larger, more active, organisms such as insects, fish and mammals, cannot rely on diffusion alone. Cells, often deep within their bodies, are metaboli-

Type of organism	single-celled	cnidarians (jellyfish and sea anemones)	insects	green plants	fish	mammals
Size range	all micro-scopic	some microscopic, some up to 60 cm	less than 1 mm to 13 cm	1 mm to 150 m	12 mm to 10 m	35 mm to 34 m
Example	*Paramecium*	sea anemone	locust	*Pelargonium*	goldfish	human
Level of activity	move in search of food	jellyfish swim slowly; anemones are sedentary and move very slowly	move actively; many fly	no movement of whole plant; parts such as leaves may move slowly	move actively	move actively
Type of transport system	no specialised transport system	no specialised transport system	blood system with pumps	xylem and phloem make up transport system; no pump	blood system with pump	blood system with pump

● *Table 1.1*

cally very active, with requirements for rapid supplies of nutrients and oxygen, and with relatively large amounts of waste products to be removed. These organisms have well-organised transport systems, with pumps to keep fluid moving through them. Plants, although large, are less metabolically active than these groups of animals, and, as you will see in chapter 3, have evolved a very different type of transport system, with no obvious pump to keep fluids moving.

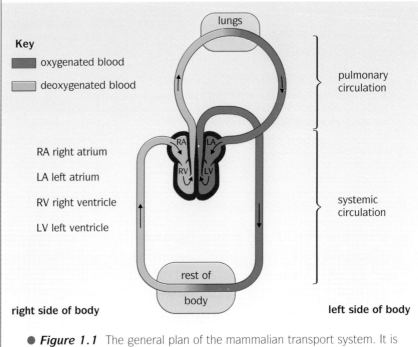

Key
■ oxygenated blood
▨ deoxygenated blood

RA right atrium
LA left atrium
RV right ventricle
LV left ventricle

lungs

pulmonary circulation

systemic circulation

rest of body

right side of body   **left side of body**

● *Figure 1.1* The general plan of the mammalian transport system. It is viewed as though looking at someone facing you.

The cardiovascular system

Figure 1.1 shows the general layout of the main transport system of mammals, that is the blood system or **cardiovascular system**. It is made up of a pump, the **heart**, and a system of interconnecting tubes, the **blood vessels**. The blood always remains within these vessels, and so the system is known as a *closed* blood system.

If you trace the journey of the blood around the body, beginning in the left ventricle of the heart, you will find that the blood travels twice through the heart on one complete 'circuit'. Blood is pumped out of the left ventricle into the **aorta** *(figure 1.3)*, and travels from there to all parts of the body except the lungs. It returns to the right side of the heart in the **vena cava**, and is then pumped out of the right ventricle into the **pulmonary arteries**, which carry it to the lungs. The final part of the journey is along the **pulmonary veins**, which return it to the left side of the heart. This is known as a **double circulatory system**.

SAQ 1.2

Figure 1.2 shows the general layout of the circulatory system of a fish.

a How does this differ from the circulatory system of a mammal?

b Suggest the possible advantages of the design of the mammalian circulatory system over that of a fish.

c Mammals are endothermic organisms; they produce heat inside their bodies, from respiration, to keep their body temperature constant. This temperature is normally higher than that of their surroundings. Most fish are exothermic organisms; they do not keep their body temperature constant. Suggest a possible link between this difference in fish and mammals and the difference in the layout of their circulatory systems.

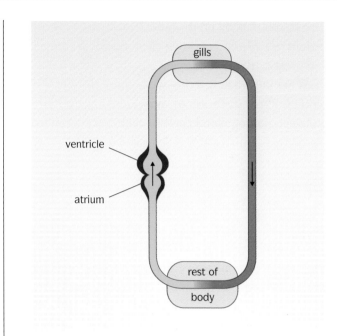

● **Figure 1.2** The general plan of the transport system of a fish.

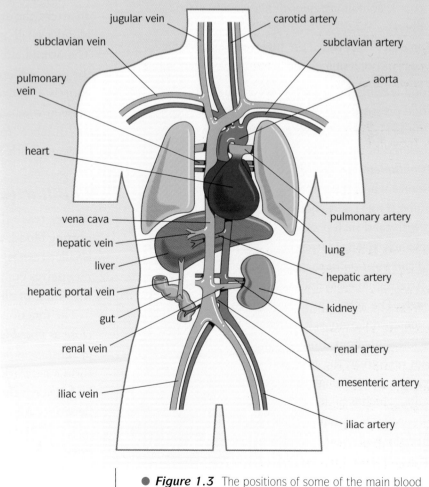

● **Figure 1.3** The positions of some of the main blood vessels in the human body.

The vessels making up the blood system are of three main types. *Figure 1.4* shows these vessels in transverse section. Vessels carrying blood away from the heart are known as **arteries**, while those carrying blood towards the heart are **veins**. Linking arteries and veins, taking blood close to almost every cell in the body, are tiny vessels called **capillaries**.

Arteries

The function of arteries is *to transport blood, swiftly and at high pressure, to the tissues*.

The structure of the wall of an artery enables it to perform this function efficiently. Arteries and veins have walls made up of three layers :

- an inner **endothelium** (lining tissue), made up of a layer of flat cells fitting together like jigsaw pieces: this layer is very smooth, minimising friction with the moving blood;
- a middle layer called the **tunica media** ('middle coat'), containing smooth muscle and elastic fibres;
- an outer layer called the **tunica externa** ('outer coat'), containing elastic fibres and collagen fibres.

Blood leaving the heart is at a very high pressure. Blood pressure in the human aorta may be around 120 mm Hg, or 16 kPa. (Blood pressure is still measured in the old units of mm Hg. This stands for *millimetres of mercury*, and refers to the distance which mercury is pushed up the arm of a U-tube. 1 mm Hg is equivalent to about 0.13 kPa.) To withstand such pressure, artery walls must be extremely strong. This is achieved by the *thickness* and *composition* of the artery wall.

Arteries have the thickest walls of any blood vessels. The aorta, the largest artery, has an overall diameter of 2.5 cm as it leaves the heart, and a wall thickness of about 2 mm. Although this may not seem very great, the composition of the wall provides great strength and resilience. The tunica media, which is by far the thickest part of the wall, contains large amounts of elastic fibres. These allow the wall to stretch as pulses of blood surge through at high pressure. Arteries further away from the heart have fewer elastic fibres in the tunica media, but have more muscle fibres.

SAQ 1.3

a Suggest why arteries close to the heart have more elastic fibres in their walls than arteries further away from the heart.

b In the disease atherosclerosis, or 'hardening of the arteries', layers of cholesterol build up inside artery walls, reducing their elasticity. Why is this dangerous?

The elasticity of artery walls is important in allowing them to 'give' as the blood surges through, so reducing the likelihood that they will burst. This elasticity also has another very important function. Blood is pumped out of the heart in pulses, rushing out at high pressure as the ventricles contract, and slowing as the ventricles relax. The artery walls stretch as the high pressure blood surges into them, and then recoil inwards as the pressure drops. Therefore, as blood at high pressure enters an artery, the artery becomes wider, reducing the pressure a little. As blood at lower pressure enters an artery, the artery wall recoils inwards, giving the blood a small 'push' and raising the pressure a little. The overall effect is to produce some smoothing of the flow of blood. However, the arteries are not entirely effective in achieving this: if you feel your pulse in your wrist, you can feel the artery, even at this distance from your heart, being stretched outwards with each surge of blood from the heart.

Capillaries

As they reach the tissue to which they are transporting blood, arteries branch into smaller and smaller vessels, called **arterioles**. The arterioles themselves continue to branch, eventually forming the tiniest of all blood vessels, **capillaries**.

The function of capillaries is to *take blood as close as possible to all cells, allowing rapid transfer of substances between cells and blood*. Capillaries form a network throughout every tissue in the body except the cornea and cartilage. Such networks are sometimes called **capillary beds**.

SAQ 1.4

Suggest why there are no blood capillaries in the cornea. How might the cornea be supplied with its requirements?

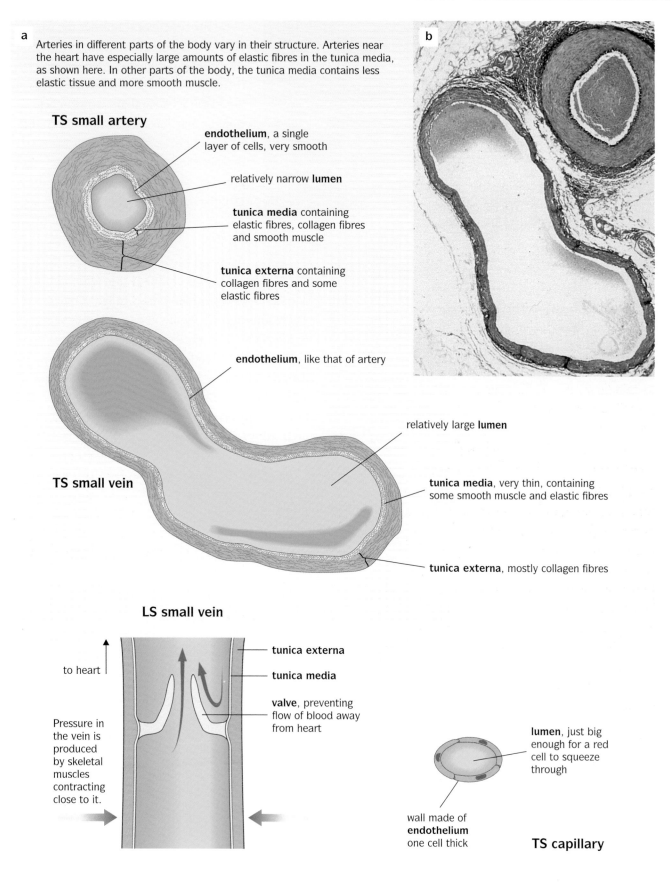

a Arteries in different parts of the body vary in their structure. Arteries near the heart have especially large amounts of elastic fibres in the tunica media, as shown here. In other parts of the body, the tunica media contains less elastic tissue and more smooth muscle.

TS small artery

endothelium, a single layer of cells, very smooth

relatively narrow **lumen**

tunica media containing elastic fibres, collagen fibres and smooth muscle

tunica externa containing collagen fibres and some elastic fibres

TS small vein

endothelium, like that of artery

relatively large **lumen**

tunica media, very thin, containing some smooth muscle and elastic fibres

tunica externa, mostly collagen fibres

LS small vein

to heart

Pressure in the vein is produced by skeletal muscles contracting close to it.

tunica externa

tunica media

valve, preventing flow of blood away from heart

lumen, just big enough for a red cell to squeeze through

wall made of **endothelium** one cell thick

TS capillary

● *Figure 1.4*   **a** The structure of arteries, veins and capillaries.   **b** Micrograph of transverse sections of an artery and a vein.

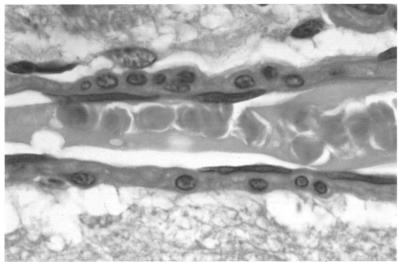

● **Figure 1.5** Micrograph of a blood capillary containing red blood cells, which are stained pink. The cells with dark purple nuclei are the endothelium of the capillary wall. During the preparation of the slide the blood plasma (light purple) has contracted, leaving white spaces inside the capillary

The small size of capillaries is obviously of great importance in allowing them to bring blood as closely as possible to each group of cells in the body. A human capillary is approximately 7 μm in diameter, about the same size as a red blood cell (*figure 1.5*). Moreover, their walls are extremely thin, made up of a single layer of endothelial cells. As red blood cells carrying oxygen squeeze through a capillary, they are brought to within as little as 1 μm of the cells outside the capillary which need the oxygen.

In most capillaries, there are tiny gaps, around 10 nm wide, between the individual cells making up the endothelium. As you will see, these gaps are important in allowing some components of the blood to seep through into the spaces between the cells in all the tissues of the body. These components form tissue fluid. The capillaries supplying the brain, however, do not have such gaps; there is a continuous wall which limits the substances which can pass from the blood into brain cells, forming a 'blood–brain barrier'. In contrast, the endothelial cells of the capillaries in the glomeruli of the kidney not only have gaps *between* them, but also holes *in* them, so speeding up the flow of fluid from the blood in the capillary into the renal capsule.

By the time blood reaches the capillaries, it has already lost a great deal of the pressure originally supplied to it by the contraction of the ventricles. As blood enters a capillary from an arteriole, it may have a pressure of around 35 mm Hg or 4.7 kPa; by the time it reaches the far end of the capillary, the pressure will have dropped to around 10 mm Hg or 1.3 kPa.

Veins

As blood leaves a capillary bed, the capillaries gradually join with one another, forming larger vessels called **venules**. These join to form **veins**. The function of veins is *to return blood to the heart*.

By the time blood enters a vein, its pressure has dropped to a very low value. In humans, a typical value for venous blood pressure is about 5 mm Hg or less. This very low pressure means that there is no need for veins to have thick walls. They have the same three layers as arteries, but the tunica media is much thinner, and has far fewer elastic fibres and muscle fibres.

The low blood pressure in veins creates a problem: how can this blood be persuaded to return to the heart? This problem is perhaps most obvious if you consider how blood can return from your legs. Left to its own devices, the blood in your leg veins would 'sink down' to its lowest level and accumulate in your feet. However, many of the veins run within, or very close to, various muscles. Whenever you tense your leg muscles, these squeeze inwards on the veins in your legs, temporarily raising the pressure within them.

This in itself would not help to push the blood back towards the heart; it would just squidge up and down as you walked. To keep the blood flowing in the right direction, veins contain half-moon valves, or **semilunar valves**, formed from their endothelium (*figure 1.4*). These valves allow blood to move towards the heart, but not away from it. Thus, when you contract your leg muscles, the blood in the veins is squeezed *up* through these valves, but cannot pass *down* through them.

SAQ 1.5

Suggest reasons for each of the following.

a Normal venous pressure in the feet is about 25 mm Hg. When a soldier stands at attention the blood pressure in his feet rises very quickly to about 90 mm Hg.

b When you breathe in, that is when the volume of the thorax increases, blood moves through the veins towards the heart.

SAQ 1.6

Construct a table comparing the structure of arteries, veins and capillaries. Include both similarities and differences, and give reasons for the differences which you describe.

SAQ 1.7

Using *figure 1.6*, describe and explain how blood pressure varies in different parts of the circulatory system.

Tissue fluid

As blood flows through capillaries within tissues, some of the plasma leaks out through the gaps between the cells in the walls of the capillary, and seeps into the spaces between the cells of the tissues. Almost one-sixth of your body consists of spaces between your cells. These spaces are filled with this leaked plasma, which is known as **tissue fluid.**

The amount of fluid which leaves the capillary to form tissue fluid depends both on the relative *hydrostatic (fluid) pressure* and on the relative *solute concentrations* inside and outside the capillary *(figure 1.7)*.

Fluids move from areas of high hydrostatic pressure to regions of low hydrostatic pressure. The hydrostatic pressure within a capillary bed ranges, as you have seen, from around 4.7 kPa at the arterial end to 1.3 kPa at the venous end. The hydrostatic pressure of tissue fluid is less than this, and so hydrostatic pressure tends to push fluid *out of* capillaries, especially at the arterial end of the capillary bed.

Water moves, by osmosis, from regions of low solute concentration to regions of high solute concentration. (This is because a high solute concentration results in a low water potential. You can read more about this in *Foundation Biology* in this series.) Blood plasma contains large amounts of dissolved plasma proteins, and therefore has a relatively high solute concentration. Tissue fluid has a relatively low solute concentration, as it contains fewer dissolved proteins than blood plasma, and therefore water tends to move *into* capillaries from tissue fluid.

The net result of these two opposing tendencies is that fluid tends to flow out of capillaries into tissue fluid near the arterial end of a capillary bed,

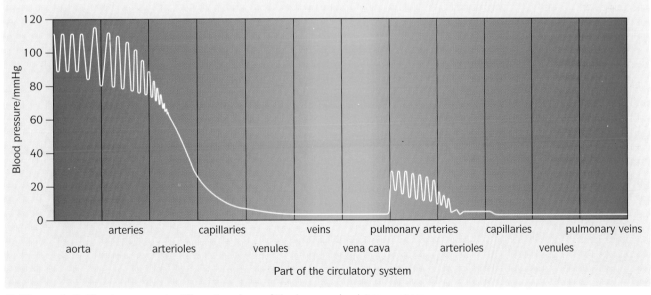

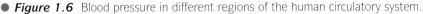

● *Figure 1.6* Blood pressure in different regions of the human circulatory system.

and into capillaries from tissue fluid near the venous end of a capillary bed. Overall, however, rather more fluid flows out of capillaries than into them, so that there is a net loss of fluid from the blood as it flows through a capillary bed.

Tissue fluid is almost identical in composition to blood plasma, which is hardly surprising as it is formed from blood plasma which has leaked from capillaries. However, it contains far fewer protein molecules than blood plasma, as these are too large to escape easily through the 10 nm-wide holes in the capillary endothelium. Red blood cells are much too large to pass through, so tissue fluid does not contain these, but some white blood cells can squeeze through, and move freely around in tissue fluid. *Table 1.2* shows the sizes of the molecules of some of the substances in blood plasma, and the relative ease with which they pass from capillaries into tissue fluid.

SAQ 1.8

Use the information in *table 1.2* to answer the following.

a How does relative molecular mass of a substance appear to correlate with the permeability of capillary walls to this substance?

b In a respiring muscle, would you expect the net diffusion of glucose to be *from* the blood plasma *to* the muscle cells, or vice versa? Explain your answer.

c Albumin is the most abundant plasma protein. Suggest why it is important that capillary walls should not be permeable to albumin.

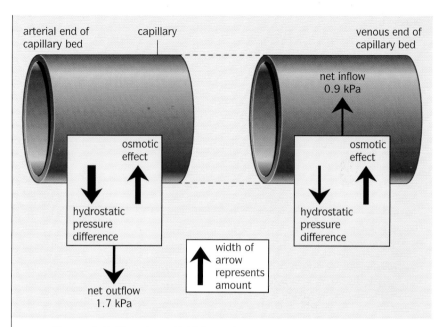

● **Figure 1.7** How tissue fluid forms from blood plasma. The hydrostatic pressure of blood is always greater than that of tissue fluid, so tends to push fluid from the blood out of the capillary. Differences in solute concentrations produce osmotic effects, which tend to push fluid from the tissue fluid into the blood. The net flow of fluid depends on the differences between these two opposing forces.

Tissue fluid forms the immediate environment of each individual body cell. It is through tissue fluid that exchanges of materials between cells and the blood occur. Within our body, many processes take place to maintain the composition of tissue fluid at a constant level, to provide an optimum environment in which cells can work. These processes contribute to the overall process of **homeostasis**, and include the regulation of glucose concentration, water, pH, metabolic wastes and temperature.

Substance	Relative molecular mass	Permeability
water	18	1.00
sodium ions	23	0.96
urea	60	0.8
glucose	180	0.6
myoglobin	17 600	0.2
haemoglobin	68 000	0.01
albumin	69 000	0.00001

The permeability to water is given a value of 1. The other values are given in proportion to that of water.

● **Table 1.2** Relative permeability of capillaries in a muscle to different substances

Lymph

As you have seen, more fluid is lost from capillaries as they pass through tissues than is returned to them. This lost fluid, about one tenth of the total amount which leaks from the capillaries, is collected up and returned to the blood system by means of a series of tubes known as **lymph vessels** or **lymphatics**.

Lymphatics are tiny, blind-ending vessels, which are found in almost all tissues of the body. The end of one of these vessels is shown in *figure 1.8*. Tissue fluid can flow into the lymphatic capillary through tiny valves, which allow it to flow in but not out. These valves are wide enough to allow large protein molecules to pass through. This is very important, as such molecules are too big to get into blood capillaries, and so cannot be taken away by the blood. If your lymphatics did not take away the protein in the tissue fluid between your cells, you could die within 24 hours. If the protein concentration and rate of loss from plasma are not in balance with the concentration and rate of loss from tissue fluid, there can be a build up of tissue fluid, called **oedema**.

SAQ 1.9

a You have seen that capillary walls are not very permeable to plasma proteins. Suggest where the protein in tissue fluid has come from.

b The disease kwashiorkor is caused by a diet which is very low in protein. The concentration of proteins in blood plasma becomes much lower than usual. One of the symptoms of kwashiorkor is oedema. Suggest why this is so.

The fluid inside lymphatics is called **lymph**. It is virtually identical to tissue fluid: it has a different name more because it is in a different place than because it is different in composition.

In some tissues, the tissue fluid, and therefore the lymph, is rather different from that in other tissues. For example, the tissue fluid and lymph in the liver have particularly high concentrations of protein. High concentrations of lipids are found in lymph in the walls of the small intestine shortly after a meal. Here, lymphatics are found in each villus, where they absorb lipids from digested food.

Lymphatics join up to form larger lymph vessels, which gradually transport the lymph back to the large veins which run just beneath the collarbone, the **subclavian veins** (*figure 1.9*). As in veins, the movement of fluid along the lymphatics is largely caused by the contraction of muscles around the vessels, and kept going in the right direction by valves. Lymph vessels also have smooth muscle in their walls, which can contract to push the lymph along. Lymph flow is very slow, and only about $100\,cm^3$ per hour flows through the largest lymph vessel, the thoracic duct, in a resting human. This contrasts with a flow rate of blood of around $80\,cm^3$ per second.

At intervals along lymph vessels are **lymph nodes**. These are involved in protection against disease. Bacteria and other unwanted particles are removed from lymph by some types of white blood cells as the lymph passes through a node, while other white blood cells within the nodes secrete antibodies.

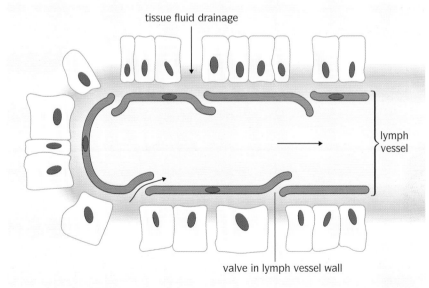

tissue fluid drainage

lymph vessel

valve in lymph vessel wall

● **Figure 1.8** Drainage of tissue fluid into a lymph vessel.

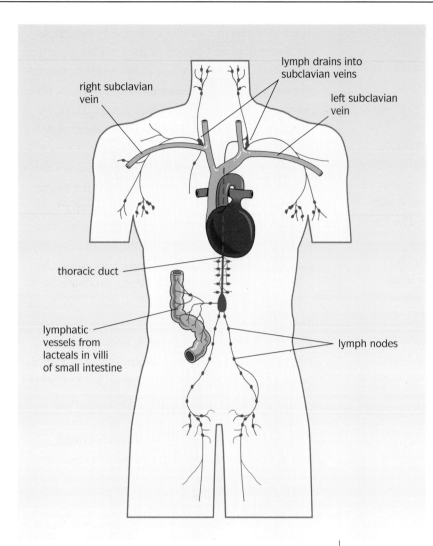

● **Figure 1.9** The human lymphatic system.

Blood

You have about 5 dm³ of blood in your body, weighing about 5 kg. Within this blood, you will have around 2.5×10^{13} red blood cells, 5×10^{11} white blood cells and 6×10^{12} platelets. These cells float in a pale yellow fluid which is called blood plasma *(figure 1.10)*.

Red blood cells

Red blood cells are also called **erythrocytes**, which simply means 'red cells'. Their red colour is caused by the pigment **haemoglobin**, a globular protein. The main function of haemoglobin is to transport oxygen from lungs to respiring tissues. This function is described in detail on pages 14–17.

A person's first red blood cells are formed in the liver, while still a fetus inside the uterus. By the time a baby is born, the liver has stopped manufacturing red blood cells. This function has been taken over by the bone

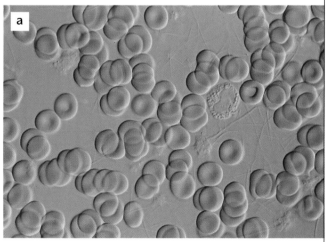

● **Figure 1.10** Micrographs of human blood.

a This photograph of unstained blood is taken with an interference contrast light microscope. Most of the cells are red blood cells. You can also see a white cell just to the right of centre (× 2500).

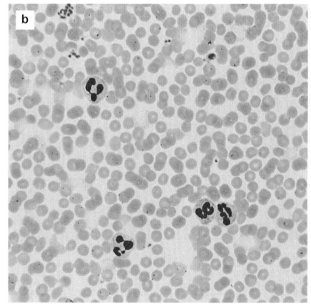

b This photograph is taken with a normal light microscope. The blood has been stained so that the nuclei of the white cells, and the platelets, are purple (× 1000).

marrow. Red blood cells continue to be made in the bone marrow, at first in the long bones such as the humerus and femur, and then increasingly in the skull, ribs, pelvis and vertebrae, throughout life. The red blood cells do not live long; their membranes become more and more fragile and eventually rupture within some 'tight spot' in the circulatory system, often inside the spleen.

SAQ 1.10

Assuming that you have 2.5×10^{13} red blood cells in your body, that the average life of a blood cell is 120 days, and that the number of red blood cells remains constant, calculate how many new blood cells must be made, on average, in your bone marrow each day.

The structure of a red blood cell (*figure 1.11*) is unusual in three ways.

■ **Red blood cells are very small.** The diameter of a human red blood cell is about 7 μm, compared with the diameter of an 'average' liver cell of 40 μm. This small size means that no haemoglobin molecule within the cell is very far from the cell's surface membrane, and can therefore quickly exchange oxygen with the fluid outside the cell. It also means that capillaries can be only 7 μm wide and still allow red blood cells to

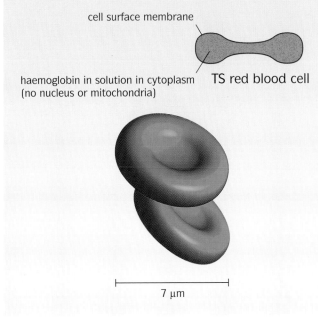

cell surface membrane

haemoglobin in solution in cytoplasm
(no nucleus or mitochondria)

TS red blood cell

7 μm

● *Figure 1.11* Red blood cells.

squeeze through them, so bringing oxygen as close as possible to cells which require it.

■ **Red blood cells are shaped like a biconcave disc.** The 'dent' in each side of a red blood cell, like its small size, increases the amount of surface area in relation to the volume of the cell, giving it a large surface area–volume ratio. This large surface area means that oxygen can diffuse quickly into or out of the cell.

■ **Red blood cells have no nucleus, no mitochondria and no endoplasmic reticulum.** The lack of these organelles means that there is more room for haemoglobin, so maximising the amount of oxygen which can be carried by each red blood cell.

SAQ 1.11

Which of these functions could, or could not, be carried out by a red blood cell? In each case, briefly justify your answer.

a Anaerobic respiration
b Aerobic respiration
c Protein synthesis
d Cell division
e Lipid synthesis
f Active transport

White blood cells

White blood cells are sometimes known as **leucocytes**, which just means 'white cells'. There are many different kinds each performing a different function in connection with protection against pathogenic (disease-producing) organisms, or the destruction of damaged cells within the body. There is no need, within this module, for you to know any detail concerning the structure and function of leucocytes, but you should be able to distinguish them from red blood cells in a blood sample. Their distinguishing features are:

■ they all have a nucleus, although the shape of this varies in different types of leucocytes;

■ most of them are larger than red blood cells, although one type, lymphocytes, may be slightly smaller;

■ they are either spherical or irregular in shape, never looking like a biconcave disc (*figure 1.12*).

There are far fewer white blood cells than red in a given volume of blood.

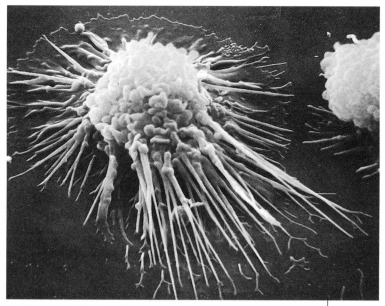

● **Figure 1.12** Scanning electron micrograph of a mammalian white blood cell (× 2500).

Platelets

Platelets, like red and white blood cells, are formed within the bone marrow. Each platelet is formed when a small part of a large cell in the bone marrow breaks off, and so consists of a small piece of cytoplasm surrounded by a cell membrane. Platelets have an even shorter life-span than red blood cells, most surviving for only about 10 days. They are very small, normally about 3 μm in diameter.

Platelets are metabolically active. Although they have no nucleus they contain mitochondria, and so can synthesise ATP both aerobically and anaerobically. They also contain enzymes which enable them to make substances called **prostaglandins**. Prostaglandins are 'local hormones', produced and released by platelets in many different situations, for example after injury to tissues. There is much current research into the roles of prostaglandins. They seem to have a very wide range of roles, for example in regulating the dilation or contraction of blood vessels, and in uterine contraction.

Platelets are of great importance in blood clotting. Their cell surface membrane has glycoproteins on its outer surface. These adhere to collagen fibres or to damaged endothelial cells within blood vessels, but not to undamaged ones. When this happens, the platelets swell, become

irregularly shaped and release ADP and a chemical called thromboxane which stimulates other platelets to behave in a similar way. The result is a collection of sticky, swollen platelets, all adhering to each other and to the damaged blood vessel wall, forming a **platelet plug**.

If the wound is small, a platelet plug may be all that is needed to seal the damaged blood vessel. If the wound is larger, then a **blood clot** may be formed. A blood clot results when the soluble protein **fibrinogen**, which is always present in blood plasma, is converted into the insoluble, fibrous protein **fibrin**, as a result of a chain of chemical reactions that take place in the blood plasma *(figure 1.13a)*. Platelets are involved in this process. They release a substance called 'cofactor 3' which is essential for some of the steps in the pathway. The fibrin forms a mesh of fibres across the wound, in which red blood cells and yet more platelets become trapped, sealing the wound, preventing blood loss and limiting the chances of pathogenic organisms entering the blood from outside *(figure 1.13b)*.

Oxygen and respiration

A major role of the cardiovascular system is to transport oxygen from the gas exchange surfaces of the alveoli in the lungs to tissues all over the body. Body cells need a constant supply of oxygen, in order to be able to carry out aerobic respiration.

The reactions of respiration begin in the cytoplasm of cells, where glucose is gradually broken down to **pyruvate** *(figure 1.14)*. This process is called **glycolysis**. Glycolysis releases sufficient energy from each glucose molecule to synthesise two **ATP** molecules from ADP. ATP, or **adenosine triphosphate**, is the 'energy currency' of all living cells, and each cell must produce a continuous supply of ATP for itself in order to maintain its life processes.

Glycolysis does not require oxygen. However, if oxygen is available within a cell, then the pyruvate produced in glycolysis moves into a mitochondrion. Here, the pyruvate combines with coenzyme A to

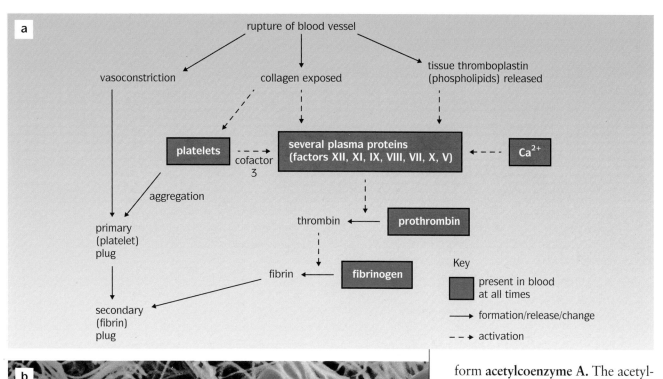

a An outline of the mechanism of blood clotting.

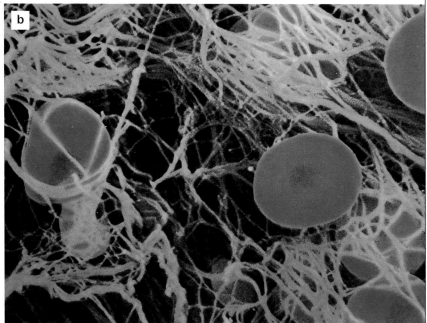

● *Figure 1.13*

a An outline of the mechanism of blood clotting. Damage to a blood vessel and tissues releases two activators of clotting. **Collagen** is exposed to blood and damaged cell membranes release **phospholipids**. These chemicals set up several complex chains of events involving a number of plasma proteins known as blood clotting factors. The end-results are aggregation of platelets and the formation of the insoluble fibrous protein fibrin from soluble fibrinogen. Fibrin fibres are precipitated across the wound, trapping blood cells and, along with the aggregated platelets, form a stable plug or blood clot.

b Scanning electron micrograph of a blood clot. The red cells are caught up in a network of fibrin fibres (× 9000).

form **acetylcoenzyme A.** The acetyl-coenzyme A then enters a series of reactions known as the **Krebs cycle**, during which carbon dioxide and hydrogen are removed from it. The carbon dioxide is released as a waste product. It diffuses into a capillary close to the respiring cell and is transported to the lungs for excretion. The hydrogen is instantly picked up by a coenzyme called **nicotinamide adenine dinucleotide**, or (more comfortably) **NAD.** The NAD then passes the hydrogen along a series of molecules known as **cytochromes**. These are able to extract energy from the process and use it to synthesise ATP. Finally, the hydrogen is handed on to oxygen, to produce water. It is for this purpose, and this purpose only, that oxygen is required by the body.

If glycolysis alone takes place, one glucose molecule can be used to synthesise two ATP molecules. However, if oxygen is available, then the Krebs cycle can run, and a total of 38 ATP molecules can be made using the energy from one glucose molecule. For most cells, a supply of oxygen is critical if they are to produce sufficient quantities of ATP to fuel whatever energy-requiring processes they are performing.

You can read more about glycolysis, the Krebs cycle and the synthesis of ATP in *Central Concepts in Biology* in this series.

Haemoglobin

Oxygen is transported around the body inside red blood cells in combination with the protein **haemoglobin.** Haemoglobin is a globular protein, and its structure is shown in *figure 1.15*. Although it is a fairly large molecule, it is small enough to be able to pass through the filtration membrane of the renal capsule in the kidneys, and would therefore be lost in the urine if it was simply free in the blood plasma rather than confined within red blood cells.

Each haemoglobin molecule is made up of four polypeptide chains, and each chain contains one haem group. Each haem group can combine with one oxygen molecule, O_2. Overall, then, each haemoglobin molecule can combine with four oxygen molecules (eight oxygen atoms).

$$\underset{\text{haemoglobin}}{\text{Hb}} + \underset{\text{oxygen}}{4O_2} \rightleftharpoons \underset{\text{oxyhaemoglobin}}{\text{HbO}_8}$$

SAQ 1.12

In an adult healthy human, the amount of haemoglobin in $1\,dm^3$ of blood is about $150\,g$.

a Given that 1 g of pure haemoglobin can combine with $1.3\,cm^3$ of oxygen at body temperature, how much oxygen can be carried in $1\,dm^3$ of blood?

b At body temperature, the solubility of oxygen in water is approximately $0.025\,cm^3$ of oxygen per cm^3 of water. Assuming that blood plasma is mostly water, how much oxygen could be carried in $1\,dm^3$ of blood if we had no haemoglobin?

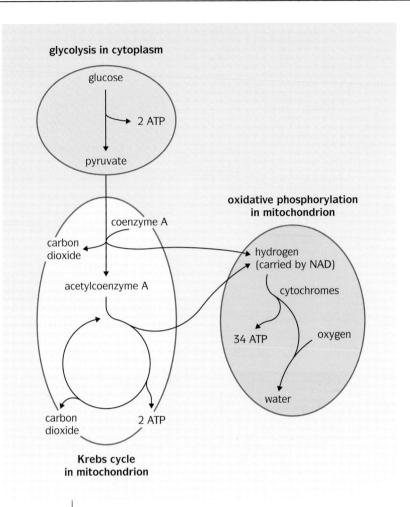

● **Figure 1.14** An outline of the pathways in aerobic respiration. These processes are described in more detail in *Central Concepts in Biology* in this series.

The haemoglobin dissociation curve

A molecule whose function is to transport oxygen from one part of the body to another must be able not only to *pick up* oxygen at the lungs, but also to *release* oxygen within respiring tissues. Haemoglobin performs this task superbly.

To find out how haemoglobin behaves at different concentrations of oxygen, haemoglobin is extracted from blood. Samples of haemoglobin are then exposed to different concentrations, or **partial pressures,** of oxygen. The amount of oxygen which combines with each sample of haemoglobin is then measured. The maximum amount of oxygen with which a sample can possibly combine is given a

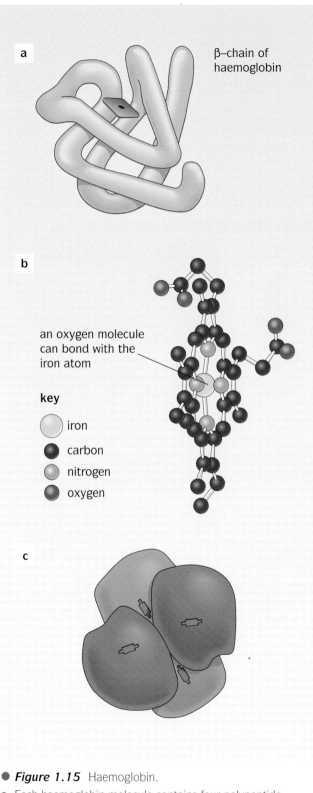

● **Figure 1.15** Haemoglobin.

a Each haemoglobin molecule contains four polypeptide chains, one of which is shown here. Each polypeptide chain contains a haem group, shown in red.

b The haem group contains an iron ion which can bond reversibly with an oxygen molecule.

c The complete haemoglobin molecule is nearly spherical.

value of 100%. A sample of haemoglobin which has combined with this maximum amount of oxygen is said to be **saturated**. The amounts with which identical samples combine at lower oxygen partial pressures are then expressed as a percentage of this maximum value. *Table 1.3* shows a series of results from such an investigation.

The percentage saturation of each sample can be plotted against the partial pressure of oxygen to obtain the curve shown in *figure 1.16*. This is known as a **dissociation curve**.

SAQ 1.13

Use the dissociation curve in *figure 1.16* to answer these questions.

a (i) The partial pressure of oxygen in the alveoli of the lungs is about 12 kPa. What is the percentage saturation of haemoglobin in the capillaries in the lungs?

(ii) If one gram of fully saturated haemoglobin is combined with 1.3 cm³ of oxygen, how much oxygen will one gram of haemoglobin in the capillaries in the lungs be combined with?

b (i) The partial pressure of oxygen in an actively respiring muscle is about 2 kPa. What is the percentage saturation of haemoglobin in the capillaries of such a muscle?

(ii) How much oxygen will one gram of haemoglobin in the capillaries of this muscle be combined with?

From the dissociation curve, you can see that at low partial pressures of oxygen, the percentage saturation of haemoglobin is very low: that is the haemoglobin is combined with only a very little oxygen. At high partial pressures of oxygen, the percentage saturation of haemoglobin is very high: that is it is combined with large amounts of oxygen.

What does this mean within the body? Consider the haemoglobin within a red blood cell in a capillary in the lungs. Here, where the partial pressure of oxygen is high, this haemoglobin will be 95–7% saturated with oxygen: that is almost every haemoglobin molecule will be combined with its full complement of eight oxygen atoms. In an actively respiring muscle, on the other hand, where the partial pressure of oxygen is low, the haemoglobin

Partial pressure of oxygen/kPa	1	2	3	4	5	6	7	8	9	10	11	12	13	14
Saturation of haemoglobin/%	8.5	24.0	43.0	57.5	71.5	80.0	85.5	88.0	92.0	94.0	95.5	96.5	97.5	98.0

● *Table 1.3*

will be about 20–5% saturated with oxygen: that is the haemoglobin is carrying, on average, only a quarter of the oxygen which it is capable of carrying. This means that haemoglobin coming from the lungs carries a lot of oxygen; as it reaches a muscle it releases around three-quarters of it. This released oxygen diffuses out of the red blood cell and into the muscle where it can be used in respiration.

The S-shaped curve

The shape of the haemoglobin dissociation curve can be explained by the behaviour of a haemoglobin molecule as it combines with or loses oxygen molecules.

Oxygen molecules combine with the iron atoms in the haem groups of a haemoglobin molecule. You will remember that each haemoglobin molecule has four haem groups. When an oxygen molecule combines with one haem group, the whole haemoglobin molecule is slightly distorted. The distortion makes it easier for a second oxygen molecule to combine with a second haem group. This in turn makes it easier for a third oxygen molecule to combine with a third haem group. It is a little harder for the fourth and final oxygen molecule to combine.

The shape of the curve reflects this behaviour. Up to an oxygen partial pressure of around 2 kPa, on average only one oxygen molecule is combined with each haemoglobin molecule. Once this oxygen molecule is combined, however, it becomes successively easier for the second and third oxygen molecules to combine, so the curve rises very steeply. Over this part of the curve, a *small* change in the partial pressure of oxygen causes a *very large* change in the amount of oxygen which is carried by the haemoglobin.

The Bohr shift

The behaviour of haemoglobin in picking up oxygen at the lungs, and readily releasing it when it finds itself in conditions of low oxygen partial pressure, is exactly what is needed. But, in fact, it is even better at this than is shown by the dissociation curve in *figure 1.16*. This is because the amount of oxygen it carries is affected not only by the partial pressure of *oxygen*, but also by the partial pressure of *carbon dioxide*.

Carbon dioxide is continually produced by respiring cells. It diffuses from the cells, and into blood plasma, from where some of it diffuses into the red blood cells. In the cytoplasm of red blood cells

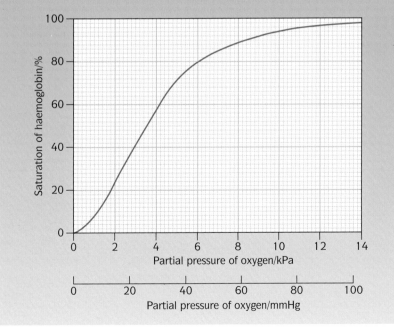

● *Figure 1.16* The haemoglobin dissociation curve.

is an enzyme, **carbonic anhydrase**. This enzyme catalyses the following reaction:

$$CO_2 + H_2O \underset{\text{carbonic anhydrase}}{\rightleftharpoons} H_2CO_3$$

carbon dioxide   water   carbonic acid

The carbonic acid dissociates:

$$H_2CO_3 \rightleftharpoons H^+ + HCO_3^-$$

carbonic acid   hydrogen ion   hydrogencarbonate ion

Haemoglobin readily combines with these hydrogen ions, forming **haemoglobinic acid, HHb**. In so doing, it releases the oxygen which it is carrying.

The net result of this reaction is two-fold.

- *Firstly*, the haemoglobin mops up the hydrogen ions which are formed when carbon dioxide dissolves and dissociates. A high concentration of hydrogen ions means a low pH; if the hydrogen ions were left in solution the blood would be very acidic. By removing the hydrogen ions from solution, haemoglobin helps to maintain the pH of the blood close to neutral. It is acting as a **buffer**.
- *Secondly*, the presence of a high partial pressure of carbon dioxide causes haemoglobin to release

oxygen. This is called the **Bohr effect**, after Christian Bohr who discovered it in 1904. It is exactly what is needed. High concentrations of carbon dioxide are found in actively respiring tissues, which need oxygen; these high carbon dioxide concentrations cause haemoglobin to release its oxygen even more readily than it would otherwise do.

If a dissociation curve is drawn for haemoglobin at a high partial pressure of carbon dioxide, it looks like the lower curve in *figure 1.17*. At each partial pressure of oxygen, the haemoglobin is less saturated than it would be at a low partial pressure of carbon dioxide. The curve therefore lies below, and to the right of, the 'normal' curve.

Carbon dioxide carriage

The description of the Bohr effect above explains one way in which carbon dioxide is carried in the blood. From the second equation, you can see that the carbon dioxide ends up as hydrogencarbonate ions, HCO_3^-. These are initially formed in the cytoplasm of the red blood cell, because this is where the enzyme carbonic anhydrase is found. Most of them then diffuse out of the red blood cell into the blood plasma, where they are carried in solution. About 85% of the carbon dioxide transported by the blood is carried in this way.

Some carbon dioxide, however, does not dissociate, but remains as carbon dioxide molecules. Some of these simply dissolve in the blood plasma; about 5% of the total is carried in this form. Others diffuse into the red blood cells, but instead of undergoing the reaction catalysed by carbonic anhydrase, combine directly with the terminal amine groups of some of the haemoglobin molecules. The compound

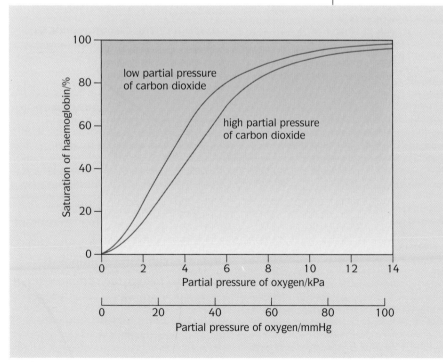

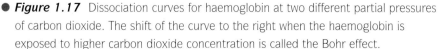

● *Figure 1.17* Dissociation curves for haemoglobin at two different partial pressures of carbon dioxide. The shift of the curve to the right when the haemoglobin is exposed to higher carbon dioxide concentration is called the Bohr effect.

formed is called **carbamino-haemoglobin**. About 10% of the carbon dioxide is carried in this way (*figure 1.18*).

When blood reaches the lungs, the reactions described above go into reverse. The relatively low concentration of carbon dioxide in the alveoli compared with that in the blood causes carbon dioxide to diffuse from the blood into the air in the alveoli, stimulating the carbon dioxide of carbamino-haemoglobin to leave the red blood cell, and hydrogencarbonate and hydrogen ions to recombine to form carbon dioxide molecules once more. This leaves the haemoglobin molecules free to combine with oxygen, ready to begin another circuit of the body.

Carboxyhaemoglobin

Despite its almost perfect design as an oxygen-transporting molecule, as described above, haemoglobin does have one property which can prove very dangerous. It combines very readily, and almost irreversibly, with carbon monoxide.

Carbon monoxide, CO, is formed when a carbon-containing compound burns incompletely. Exhaust fumes from cars contain significant amounts of carbon monoxide, as does cigarette smoke. When such fumes are inhaled, the carbon monoxide readily diffuses across the walls of the alveoli, into blood, and into red blood cells. Here it combines with the haem groups in the haemoglobin molecules, forming **carboxyhaemoglobin**.

Haemoglobin will combine with carbon monoxide 250 times more readily than it will combine with oxygen. Thus, even if the concentration of carbon monoxide in air is much lower than the concentration of oxygen, a high proportion of haemoglobin will combine with carbon monoxide. Moreover, carboxyhaemoglobin is a very stable compound; the carbon monoxide remains combined with the haemoglobin for a long time.

The result of this is that even relatively low concentrations of carbon monoxide, as low as 0.1% of the air, can cause death by asphyxiation. The victim looks very bright red, the colour of carboxyhaemoglobin. Treatment of carbon monoxide poisoning involves administration of a mixture of pure oxygen and carbon dioxide: high concentrations of oxygen to favour the combination of haemoglobin with oxygen rather than carbon monoxide, and carbon dioxide to stimulate the breathing centres in the brain (page 62).

Cigarette smoke contains up to 5% carbon monoxide. If you breathed in

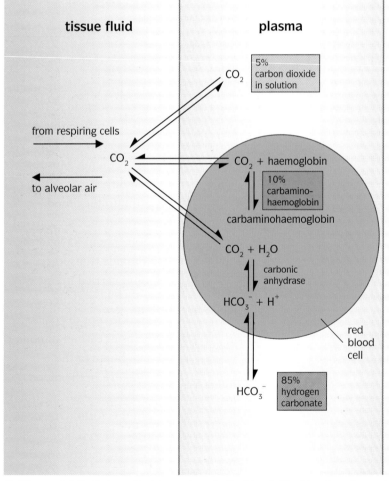

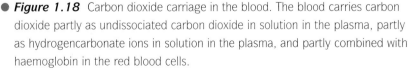

● **Figure 1.18** Carbon dioxide carriage in the blood. The blood carries carbon dioxide partly as undissociated carbon dioxide in solution in the plasma, partly as hydrogencarbonate ions in solution in the plasma, and partly combined with haemoglobin in the red blood cells.

'pure' cigarette smoke for any length of time, you would die of asphyxiation. As it is, even smokers who inhale also breathe in some normal air, so diluting the carbon monoxide levels in their lungs. Nevertheless, around 5% of the haemoglobin in a regular smoker's blood is permanently combined with carbon monoxide. This considerably reduces its oxygen-carrying capacity.

Fetal haemoglobin

A developing fetus obtains its oxygen not from its own lungs, but from its mother's blood. In the placenta, the mother's blood is brought very close to that of the fetus, allowing diffusion of various substances from mother to fetus or vice versa.

Oxygen arrives at the placenta in combination with haemoglobin, inside the mother's red blood cells. The partial pressure of oxygen in the blood vessels in the placenta is relatively low, because the fetus is respiring. The mother's haemoglobin therefore releases some of its oxygen, which diffuses from her blood into the fetus' blood.

The partial pressure of oxygen in the fetus' blood is only a little lower than that in its mother's blood. However, the haemoglobin of the fetus is different from its mother's haemoglobin. Fetal haemoglobin combines more readily with oxygen than adult haemoglobin; thus, the fetal haemoglobin will pick up oxygen which the adult haemoglobin has dropped. Fetal haemoglobin is said to have a *higher affinity* for oxygen than adult haemoglobin.

A dissociation curve for fetal haemoglobin (*figure 1.19*) shows that, at each partial pressure of oxygen, fetal haemoglobin is slightly more saturated than adult haemoglobin. The curve lies above the curve for adult haemoglobin.

Myoglobin

Myoglobin, like haemoglobin, is a red pigment which combines reversibly with oxygen. It is not found in the blood, but inside cells in some tissues of the body, especially in muscle cells. The red colour of meat is largely caused by myoglobin.

Each myoglobin molecule is made up of only one polypeptide chain, rather than the four in a haemoglobin molecule. It has just one haem group, and can combine with just one oxygen molecule. However, once combined, the oxymyoglobin molecule is very stable, and will not release its oxygen unless the partial pressure of oxygen around it is very low indeed. The curve in *figure 1.19* shows this in comparison with haemoglobin. At each partial pressure of oxygen, myoglobin has a higher percentage saturation with oxygen than haemoglobin does.

This means that myoglobin acts as an **oxygen store**. At the normal partial pressures of oxygen in a respiring muscle, haemoglobin releases its oxygen. Some of this oxygen is picked up and held tightly by myoglobin in the muscle. The myoglobin will not release this oxygen unless the oxygen concentration in the muscle drops very low, that is unless the muscle is using up oxygen at a faster rate than the haemoglobin in the blood can supply it. The oxygen held by the myoglobin is a reserve, to be used only in conditions of particularly great oxygen demand.

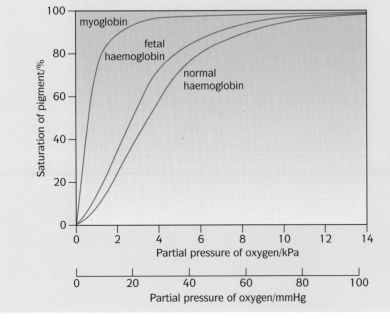

● *Figure 1.19* Dissociation curves for myoglobin and fetal haemoglobin.

SUMMARY

■ Large, active organisms such as mammals need a transport system, in which fluid driven by a pump carries oxygen and nutrients to all tissues, and removes waste products from them. Mammals have a double circulatory system.

■ Blood is carried away from the heart in arteries, passes through tissues in capillaries, and is returned to the heart in veins. Blood pressure drops gradually as it passes along this system.

■ Arteries have thick, elastic walls, to allow them to withstand high blood pressures and to smooth out the pulsed blood flow. Capillaries are only just wide enough to allow the passage of red blood cells, and have very thin walls to allow efficient and rapid transfer of materials between blood and cells. Veins have thinner walls than arteries and possess valves, to help blood at low pressure flow back to the heart.

■ Plasma leaks from capillaries to form tissue fluid. This is collected into lymphatics and returned to the blood in the subclavian veins.

■ Red blood cells carry oxygen in combination with haemoglobin. Haemoglobin picks up oxygen at high partial pressures of oxygen in the lungs, and releases it at low partial pressures of oxygen in respiring tissues. It releases oxygen more easily when carbon dioxide concentration is high. Fetal haemoglobin and myoglobin have a higher affinity for oxygen than adult haemoglobin, so they can take oxygen from adult haemoglobin.

■ Carbon dioxide is mostly carried as hydrogencarbonate ions in blood plasma, but also in combination with haemoglobin in red blood cells and dissolved as carbon dioxide molecules in blood plasma.

■ White blood cells aid in defence against disease, while platelets are involved in blood clotting.

Questions

1 Discuss the need for transport systems in multicellular animals.

2 Discuss the ways in which a red blood cell is adapted for its functions.

3 Summarise the ways in which
  a oxygen and
  b carbon dioxide
  are transported in the body of a mammal.

4 a What is the Bohr effect?
  b Why is the Bohr effect useful?
  c The magnitude of the Bohr effect differs between species. Suggest reasons for each of the following.
   • The Bohr effect in Weddell seals, which can dive to 400 m for up to 43 minutes, is large.
   • The Bohr effect in hibernating hedgehogs is low.

Chapter two

The heart

By the end of this chapter you should be able to:

1 describe the external and internal structure of the human heart;

2 describe the cardiac cycle, and interpret graphs showing pressure changes during this cycle;

3 explain the reasons for the difference in thickness of the atrial and ventricular walls, and of the left and right ventricular walls;

4 describe and explain the functioning of the atrio-ventricular valves, and of the semilunar valves in the aorta and pulmonary artery;

5 explain the role of the sinoatrial node in initiating heart beat, and the roles of the atrio-ventricular node and Purkyne fibres in coordinating the actions of the different parts of the heart;

6 explain how the rate of heart beat can be modified.

Figure 2.1 shows the appearance of a human heart, looking at it from the front of the body. The heart of an adult has a mass of around 300 g, and is about the size of your fist. It is a bag of muscle, filled with blood.

The muscle of which the heart is made is called **cardiac muscle**. *Figure 2.3* shows the structure of this type of muscle. It is made of interconnecting cells, whose cell membranes are very tightly joined together. This close contact between the muscle cells allows waves of excitation to pass easily between them, which is a very important feature of cardiac muscle, as you will see later.

Figure 2.1 also shows the blood vessels which carry blood into and out of the heart. The large, arching blood vessel is the largest artery, the **aorta**, with branches leading upwards towards the head. The other artery

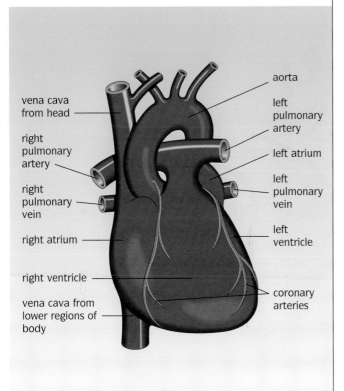

● *Figure 2.1* External appearance of a human heart, seen from the front.

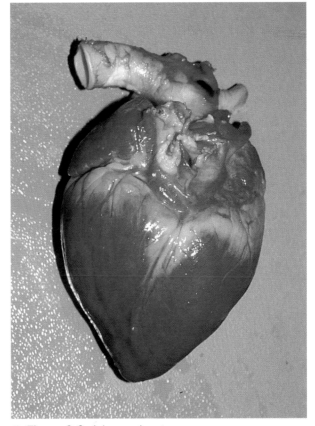

● *Figure 2.2* A human heart.

leaving the heart is the **pulmonary artery**. This, too, branches very quickly after leaving the heart, into two arteries taking blood to the right and left lungs. Running vertically on the right-hand side of the heart are the two large veins, the **venae cavae**, one bringing blood down-

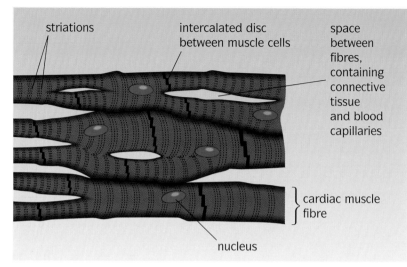

● *Figure 2.3* Cardiac muscle, as it appears under the high power of a light microscope.

wards from the head and the other bringing it upwards from the rest of the body. The **pulmonary veins** bring blood back to the heart from the left and right lungs.

On the surface of the heart, the **coronary arteries** can be seen. These branch from the aorta, and deliver oxygenated blood to the outer layers of the cardiac muscle that make up the walls of the heart.

If the heart is cut open vertically *(figure 2.4)* it can be seen to contain four chambers. The two chambers on the left of the heart

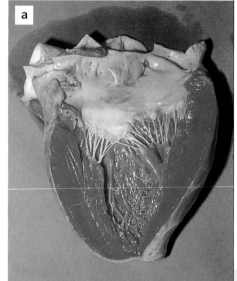

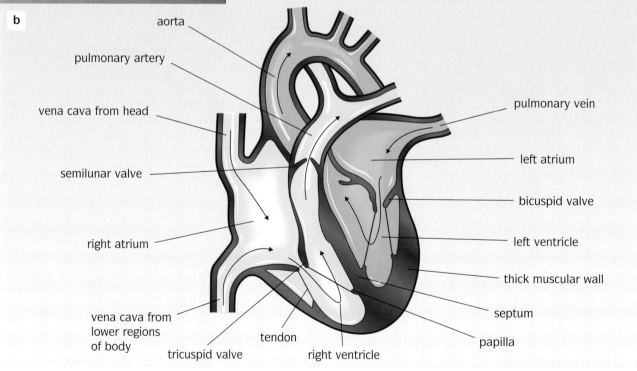

● *Figure 2.4* Vertical sections through a human heart. In the photograph, the heart has been cut through the left atrium and ventricle only.

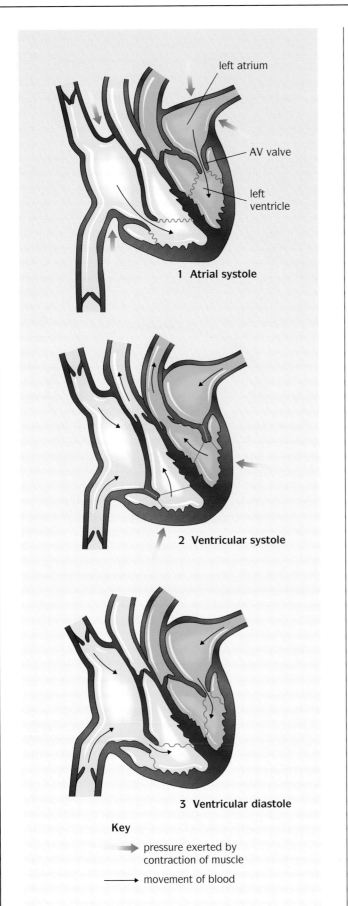

1 Atrial systole

2 Ventricular systole

3 Ventricular diastole

Key

→ pressure exerted by contraction of muscle

→ movement of blood

are completely separated from those on the right by a wall of muscle called the **septum**. Blood cannot pass through this septum; the only way for blood to get from one side of the heart to the other is to leave the heart, circulate around either the lungs or the rest of the body, and then return to the heart.

The upper chamber on each side is called an **atrium** (or sometimes an **auricle**). The two atria receive blood from the veins. You can see from the diagram that blood from the venae cavae flows into the right atrium, while blood from the pulmonary veins flows into the left atrium.

The lower chambers are **ventricles**. Blood flows into the ventricles from the atria, and is then squeezed out into the arteries. Blood from the left ventricle flows into the aorta, while blood from the right ventricle flows into the pulmonary arteries.

The atria and ventricles have valves between them, which are known as the **atrioventricular valves**. The one on the left is the **mitral** or **bicuspid valve**, and the one on the right is the **tricuspid valve**.

The cardiac cycle

Your heart beats around 70 times a minute. The **cardiac cycle** is the sequence of events which makes up one heart beat.

As the cycle is continuous, a description of it could begin anywhere. We will begin with the time when the heart is filled with blood, and the muscle in the atrial walls contracts. This stage is called **atrial systole** *(figure 2.5)*. The pressure developed

● **Figure 2.5** The cardiac cycle. Only three stages in this continuous process are shown.
1 Atrial systole Both atria contract. Blood flows from the atria into the ventricles. Backflow of blood into the veins is prevented by closure of valves in the veins.
2 Ventricular systole Both ventricles contract. The atrioventricular valves close. The semilunar valves in the aorta and pulmonary artery open. Blood flows from the ventricles into the arteries.
3 Ventricular diastole Atria and ventricles relax. Blood flows from the veins through the atria and into the ventricles.

by this contraction is not very great, because the muscular walls of the atria are only thin, but it is enough to force the blood in the atria down through the atrio-ventricular valves into the ventricles. The blood from the atria does not go back into the pulmonary veins or the venae cavae, because these have semi-lunar valves to prevent backflow.

About 0.1 second after the atria contract, the ventricles contract. This is called **ventricular systole**. The thick, muscular walls of the ventricles squeeze inwards on the blood, increasing its pressure and pushing it out of the heart. As soon as the pressure in the ventricles becomes greater than the pressure in the atria, the pressure of blood in the ventricles pushes the atrioventricular valves shut (*figure 2.6a*), preventing blood from going back into the atria. Instead, the blood rushes upwards into the aorta and the pulmonary artery, pushing open the **semilunar valves** in these vessels as it does so (*figure 2.6b*).

Ventricular systole lasts for about 0.3 second. The muscle then relaxes, and the stage called ventricular **diastole** begins (*figure 2.5*). As the muscle relaxes, the pressure in the ventricles drops. The high-pressure blood which has just been pushed into the arteries would flow back into the ventricles, but for the presence of the semilunar valves, which snap shut as the blood fills their cusps.

During diastole, as the whole of the heart muscle relaxes, blood from the veins flows into the two atria. The blood is at a very low

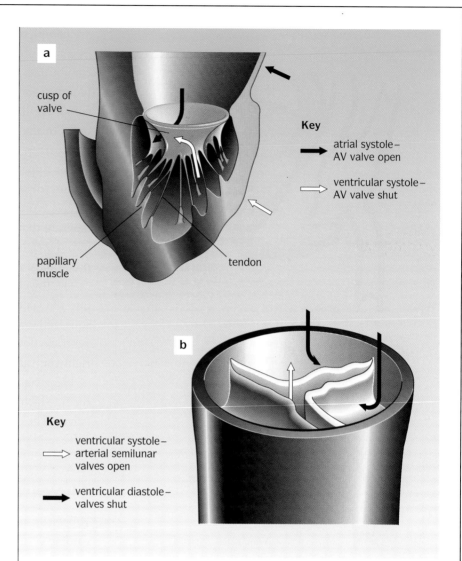

● *Figure 2.6*

a How the mitral (bicuspid) valve functions. During atrial systole (black arrow) the pressure of blood is higher in the atrium than in the ventricle and so forces the valve open. During ventricular systole (white arrow) the pressure of blood is higher in the ventricle than in the atrium. The pressure of the blood pushes up against the valve, pushing it shut. Contraction of the papillary muscles, attached to the valve by tendons, prevents the valve from being forced inside-out.

b How the semilunar valves in the aorta and pulmonary arteries function. During ventricular systole (white arrow) the pressure of the blood forces the valves open. During ventricular diastole (black arrows) the pressure of blood in the arteries is higher than in the ventricles. The pressure of the blood pushes into the cusps of the valves, squeezing them shut.

pressure, but the thin walls of the atria are easily distended, providing very little resistance to the blood flow. Some of the blood trickles downwards into the ventricles, through the atrioventricular valves. The atrial muscle then contracts, to push blood forcefully down into the ventricles, and the whole cycle begins again.

The walls of the ventricles are much thicker than the walls of the atria, because the ventricles need to develop much more force when they contract. Their contraction has to push the blood out of the heart and around the body. For the right ventricle, the force required is relatively small, as the blood goes only to the lungs, which are very close to the heart. The left ventricle, however, has to develop sufficient force to push blood around all the rest of the body. Therefore, the thickness of the muscular wall of the left ventricle is much greater than that of the right.

SAQ 2.1

Figure 2.7 shows the pressure changes in the left atrium, left ventricle and aorta throughout one cardiac cycle. Make a copy of this diagram.

a (i) How long does one heart beat (one cardiac cycle) last?

(ii) What is the heart rate represented on this graph, in beats per minute?

b The contraction of muscles in the ventricle wall causes the pressure inside the ventricle to rise. When the muscles relax, the pressure drops again.

On your copy of the diagram, mark the following periods:

(i) the time when the ventricle is contracting (ventricular systole);

(ii) the time when the ventricle is relaxing (ventricular diastole).

c The contraction of muscles in the wall of the atrium raises the pressure inside it. This pressure is also raised when blood flows into the atrium from the veins, while the atrial walls are relaxed.

On your copy of the diagram, mark the following periods:

(i) the time when the atrium is contracting (atrial systole);

(ii) the time when the atrium is relaxing (atrial diastole).

d The valves between the atria and ventricles open when the pressure of the blood in the atria is greater than that in the ventricles. They snap shut when the pressure of the blood in the ventricles is greater than that in the atria. On your diagram, mark the point at which these valves will open and close.

e The opening and closing of the semilunar valves in the aorta (and pulmonary artery) depends in a similar way on the relative pressures in the aorta and ventricles. On your diagram, mark the point at which these valves will open and close.

f The right ventricle has much less muscle in its walls than the left ventricle, and only develops about one-quarter of the pressure developed on the left side of the heart. On your diagram, draw a line to represent the probable pressure inside the right ventricle over the 1.3 seconds shown.

Control of heart beat

Cardiac muscle differs from the muscle in all other areas of the body in that it is **myogenic**. This means that it naturally contracts and relaxes: it does not need to receive impulses from a nerve to make it contract. If cardiac muscle cells are cultured in a warm, oxygenated solution containing nutrients, they contract and relax rhythmically, all by themselves.

However, the individual heart muscle cells cannot be allowed to contract at their

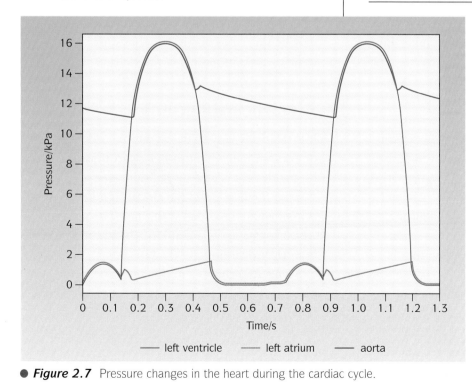

● *Figure 2.7* Pressure changes in the heart during the cardiac cycle.

own natural rhythms. If they did, parts of the heart would contract out of sequence with other parts; the sequence of the cardiac cycle would become disordered, and the heart would stop working as a pump. The heart is designed with its own built-in controlling and coordinating system.

The cardiac cycle is initiated in a specialised patch of muscle in the wall of the right atrium, called the **sinoatrial node**. It is often called the **SAN**, or **pacemaker**. The muscle cells of the SAN set the rhythm for all the other cardiac muscle cells. They have an inbuilt rhythm of contraction which is slightly faster than the rest of the heart muscle. Each time they contract, they set up an excitation wave, that is a wave of depolarisation, which spreads out rapidly over the whole of the atrial walls. The cardiac muscle in the atrial walls responds to the excitation wave by contracting, at the same rhythm as the SAN. Thus, all the muscle in both atria contracts almost simultaneously.

As you have seen, the muscles of the ventricles do not contract until the muscles of the atria have finished contracting. (You can imagine what would happen if they all contracted at once.) The heart is designed to ensure that there is a delay before the excitation wave can pass from the atria to the ventricles.

The cause of the delay is a band of fibres between the atria and ventricles which does not conduct the excitation wave. Thus, as the wave spreads out from the SAN over the atrial walls, it does not pass into the ventricle walls. The only way by which this excitation wave can spread into the ventricles is through a patch of conducting fibres, situated in the septum *(figure 2.8)*, known as the **atrioventricular node**, or AVN. The AVN picks up the excitation wave as it spreads across the atria and, after a delay of about 0.1 second, passes it on to a bunch of conducting fibres, called **Purkyne fibres**, which run down the septum between the ventricles. These transmit the excitation wave very rapidly down to the base of the septum, from where it spreads outwards and upwards through the ventricle walls. As it does so, it causes the cardiac muscle in these walls to contract, from the bottom up, so squeezing blood upwards and into the arteries.

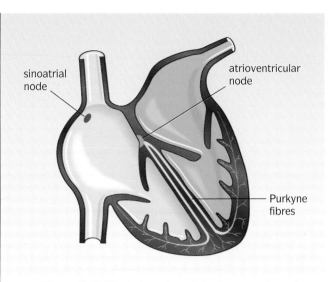

● *Figure 2.8* Vertical section of the heart to show the positions of the sinoatrial node and the atrioventricular node.

Sometimes, this coordination of contraction goes wrong. The excitation wave becomes chaotic, passing through the ventricular muscle in all directions, feeding back on itself and restimulating areas it has just left. Small sections of the cardiac muscle contract while other sections are relaxing. The result is **fibrillation**, in which the heart wall simply flutters, rather than contracting as a whole and then relaxing as a whole. Fibrillation is almost always fatal, unless treated instantly. Fibrillation may be started by an electric shock, or by damage to large areas of muscle in the walls of the heart.

Electrocardiograms

It is relatively easy to detect and record the waves of excitation flowing through heart muscle. Electrodes are placed on the skin over opposite sides of the heart, and the electrical potentials generated are recorded with time. The result, which is essentially a graph of voltage against time, is an **electrocardiogram (ECG)**.

Figure 2.9a shows a normal electrocardiogram. The part labelled **P** represents the wave of excitation sweeping over the atrial walls. The parts labelled **Q**, **R** and **S** represent the wave of excitation in the ventricle walls. The **T** section indicates the recovery of the ventricle walls.

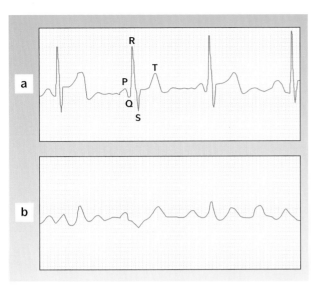

● **Figure 2.9** Electrocardiograms.
a Normal. Notice the regular, repeating pattern.
b Fibrillation.

Figure 2.9b shows an electrocardiogram from a fibrillating heart. There is no obvious regular rhythm at all. A patient in intensive care in hospital may be connected to a monitor which keeps track of the heart rhythm. If fibrillation begins, a warning sound brings a resuscitation team running. They will attempt to shock the heart out of its fibrillation by passing a strong electric current through the chest wall. This usually stops the heart completely for up to 5 seconds, after which it often begins to beat again in a controlled way. This treatment has to be carried out within one minute after fibrillation begins to have any real chance of success.

SAQ 2.2

Figure 2.9a shows a normal ECG. The paper on which the ECG was recorded was running at a speed of $25\,mm\,s^{-1}$.

a Calculate the heart rate in beats per minute.

b The time interval between **Q** and **T** is called the *contraction time*.
   (i) Suggest why it is given this name.
   (ii) Calculate the contraction time from this ECG.

c The time interval between **T** and **Q** is called the *filling time*.
   (i) Suggest why it is given this name.
   (ii) Calculate the filling time from this ECG.

d An adult male recorded his ECG at different heart rates. The contraction time and filling time were calculated from the ECGs. The results are shown in *table 2.1*.
   (i) Suggest how the man could have increased his heart rate for the purposes of the experiment.
   (ii) Present these results as a line graph, drawing both curves on the same pair of axes.
   (iii) Comment on these results.

Heart rate / beats per minute	Contraction time/s	Filling time/s
39.5	0.37	1.14
48.4	0.39	0.82
56.6	0.39	0.66
58.0	0.38	0.60
60.0	0.38	0.57
63.8	0.40	0.54
68.2	0.42	0.45
69.8	0.38	0.46
73.2	0.38	0.44
75.0	0.38	0.39
78.9	0.38	0.36
81.1	0.39	0.33
85.7	0.37	0.32
88.2	0.39	0.30

● **Table 2.1**

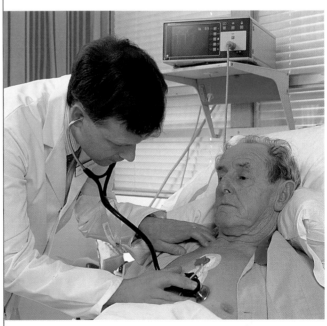

● **Figure 2.10** This patient is recovering from a heart attack in the coronary care unit of a hospital in Newcastle-upon-Tyne, England. The electrodes on his chest are connected to the heart monitor behind him, on which his heart beat is recorded.

Regulation of cardiac output

The amount of blood pumped out by the heart per minute depends on the *rate* at which it beats, and also the *volume* of blood pumped out with each beat. The number of beats per minute multiplied by the volume of blood pumped with each beat is called the **cardiac output**.

There are three ways in which the rate and degree of force with which the heart beats can be modified (*figure 2.11*):

- by changes in the volume of blood entering the heart through the veins;
- by nerves from the brain, bringing messages to the SAN;
- by hormones, especially adrenaline.

Let us look at each of these methods in turn.

By changes in the volume of blood entering the heart through the veins

Under normal conditions, this is the main factor determining cardiac output. If a larger volume of blood than usual flows into the heart, this stretches the heart walls more than usual. The heart responds by contracting faster and more forcefully.

What might cause such changes in blood volume entering the heart? One common cause is **exercise**. During exercise, muscles use large quantities of oxygen. This causes a drop in oxygen concentration in the blood vessels running through the exercising muscle. This causes the muscles in the walls of these blood vessels to relax, so that the vessels become wider and carry more blood. This in turn results in more blood flowing into the veins, and hence into the heart, which stimulates an increase in cardiac output.

By nerves from the brain, connected to the SAN

Two nerves bring messages to the SAN from the brain. They run from an area at the base of the brain, in the medulla oblongata, called the **cardiovascular centre**. One of the nerves is called the **accelerator nerve**, and an impulse along this nerve causes the SAN, and therefore the whole heart, to beat faster. The other nerve is the **vagus nerve**, which slows down the heart rate.

What causes the brain to send messages to the SAN along one of these two nerves? It could simply be that you are about to perform

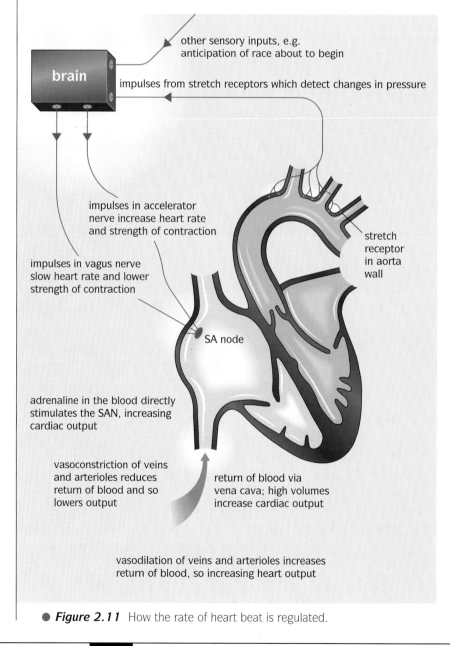

other sensory inputs, e.g. anticipation of race about to begin

brain

impulses from stretch receptors which detect changes in pressure

impulses in accelerator nerve increase heart rate and strength of contraction

stretch receptor in aorta wall

impulses in vagus nerve slow heart rate and lower strength of contraction

SA node

adrenaline in the blood directly stimulates the SAN, increasing cardiac output

vasoconstriction of veins and arterioles reduces return of blood and so lowers output

return of blood via vena cava; high volumes increase cardiac output

vasodilation of veins and arterioles increases return of blood, so increasing heart output

● *Figure 2.11* How the rate of heart beat is regulated.

some vigorous activity, such as running a race. When your brain sends signals to your muscles to begin exercise, it simultaneously sends signals along the accelerator nerve to the SAN to increase heart rate. Thus, your heart starts beating faster straight away, providing your muscles with extra oxygen even before they need it.

Another factor which can trigger signals in these nerves is the blood pressure in the aorta and carotid arteries. These vessels have **stretch receptors** in their walls. If blood pressure in the arteries is high, the stretch receptors are stimulated, and send impulses along nerves to the cardiovascular centre. This then sends impulses along the vagus nerve, which slows the rate of heart beat. On the other hand, if blood pressure is low, the cardiovascular centre sends impulses along the accelerator nerve, speeding the rate of heart beat.

These reactions to a rise or fall in arterial pressure help to regulate blood pressure. For example, if there is a rapid loss of blood after an accident, then blood pressure in the arteries will drop. This will produce an increase in heart rate, which will help to restore arterial pressure to somewhere near normal.

By hormones, especially adrenaline

Adrenaline is secreted from the adrenal glands in times of stress or need for action, and is carried in the blood to all areas of the body. It stimulates the SAN to increase its rate, so increasing the heart rate.

SUMMARY

■ The human heart, like that of all mammals, has two atria and two ventricles. Blood enters the atria and leaves from the ventricles. A septum separates the right side, which contains deoxygenated blood, from the left side, which contains oxygenated blood. Valves in the veins, between the atria and ventricles and in the entrances to the aorta and pulmonary artery prevent backflow of blood.

■ The heart is made of cardiac muscle and is myogenic. The sinoatrial node sets the pace of contraction for the muscle in the heart. Excitation waves spread from the SAN across the atria, causing their walls to contract. A non-conducting barrier prevents these excitation waves from spreading directly into the ventricles, thus delaying their contraction. The excitation wave travels to the ventricles via the atrio-ventricular node and the Purkyne fibres, which run down through the septum before spreading out into the walls of the ventricles. Both sides of the heart contract and relax at the same time. The contraction phase is called systole, and the relaxation phase diastole.

■ The rate of heart beat is controlled by the pressure of blood flowing into it through the veins, by the accelerator and vagus nerves from the cardiovascular centre in the brain, and by hormones such as adrenaline.

Questions

1 Describe what happens during one heart beat. Include both a description of the way in which the beating of the different parts of the heart are synchronised, and of how the blood is moved through the heart.

2 The following factors can each cause an increase in heart rate. Suggest the possible mechanisms by which this increase might occur.

   a Fear

   b Anaemia

Transport in plants

Plant cells, like animal cells, need a regular supply of oxygen and nutrients. However, their requirements differ from those of animals in several ways, both in the nature of the nutrients and gases required and the rate at which these need to be supplied. Some of the particular requirements of plant cells are:

■ **Carbon dioxide** Photosynthetic plant cells require a supply of carbon dioxide during daylight.

■ **Oxygen** All plant cells require a supply of oxygen for respiration, but cells which are actively photosynthesising produce more than enough oxygen for their own needs. Cells which are not photosynthesising need to take in oxygen from their environment, but they do not respire at such a high rate as animals and therefore do not need such a rapid oxygen supply.

■ **Organic nutrients** Some plant cells make many of their own organic food materials, such as glucose, by photosynthesis. However, many plant cells do not photosynthesise and need to be supplied with organic nutrients from photosynthetic cells.

■ **Inorganic ions and water** These are taken up from the soil, by roots, and are transported to all regions of the plant.

The energy requirements of plant cells are, on average, far lower than those of cells in a mammal such as a human. Thus, their rate of respiration, and their requirement for oxygen and glucose, is considerably less than that of mammals. They can therefore manage with a much slower transport system than the circulatory system of a mammal.

One of the main requirements of the photosynthetic regions of a plant is sunlight. In order to absorb as much sunlight as possible, plants have thin, flat leaves which present a large surface area to the Sun. In consequence, it is relatively easy for carbon dioxide and oxygen to diffuse into and out of the leaves, reaching and leaving every cell quickly enough so that there is no need for a transport system for these gases.

So, the design of a plant's transport system is quite different from that of a mammal. In fact, plants have *two* transport systems: one for carrying mainly water and inorganic ions from roots to the parts above ground, and one for carrying substances made by photosynthesis from the leaves to other areas. In neither of these systems do fluids move as rapidly as blood does in a mammal, nor is there an obvious pump such as the heart. Neither plant transport system is concerned with the transport of oxygen or carbon dioxide, which travel to and from cells and their environment by diffusion alone.

The transport of water

Figure 3.1 outlines the pathway taken by water as it is transported through a plant. Water from the soil enters a plant through its root hairs and then moves across the root into the xylem tissue in the centre. Once inside the xylem vessels, the water moves upwards through the root to the stem and from there into the leaves.

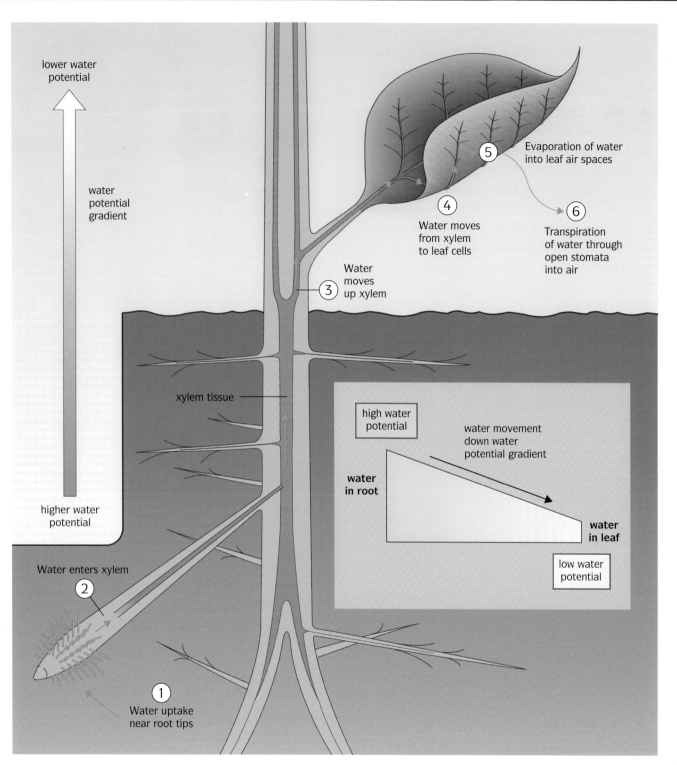

lower water
potential

water
potential
gradient

higher water
potential

Water enters xylem

②

① Water uptake
near root tips

xylem tissue

③ Water moves up xylem

④ Water moves from xylem to leaf cells

⑤ Evaporation of water into leaf air spaces

⑥ Transpiration of water through open stomata into air

high water potential

water movement down water potential gradient

water in root

water in leaf

low water potential

● *Figure 3.1* An overview of the movement of water through a plant. Water moves down a water potential gradient from the soil to the air.

Root hairs

Figure 3.2 shows the tip of a root. The tip itself is covered by a tough, protective root cap and is not permeable to water. However, just behind the tip some of the cells in the outer layer, or **epidermis**, are drawn out into long, thin extensions called **root hairs**. These reach into spaces between the soil particles from where they absorb water.

Water moves into the root hairs down a water potential gradient *(figure 3.3)*. Although soil water contains some inorganic ions in solution, it is a relatively dilute solution and so has a relatively high water potential. However, the cytoplasm and cell sap inside the root hair have considerable quantities of inorganic ions and organic substances, such as proteins and sugars, dissolved in them, and so have a relatively low water potential. Water, therefore, diffuses down this water potential gradient, through the partially permeable cell surface membrane, into the cytoplasm and vacuole of the root hair cell.

The large number of very fine root hairs provides a large surface area in contact with soil water, thus increasing the rate at which water can be absorbed. However, these root hairs are very delicate and often only function for a few days before being replaced by new ones as the root grows. Root hairs are also important for the absorption of mineral ions such as nitrate.

Many plants, especially trees, have fungal mycelium located in or on their roots forming associations called mycorrhizae (singular mycorrhiza), which serve a similar function to root hairs. The mycorrhizae act like a mass of fine roots which absorb nutrients, especially phosphate, from the soil and transport them into the plant. Some trees, if growing on poor soils, are unable to survive without these fungi. In return, the fungi receive organic nutrients from the plant.

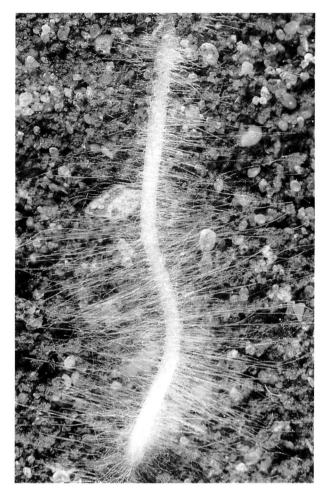

● *Figure 3.2* A root of a young radish plant showing the root hairs.

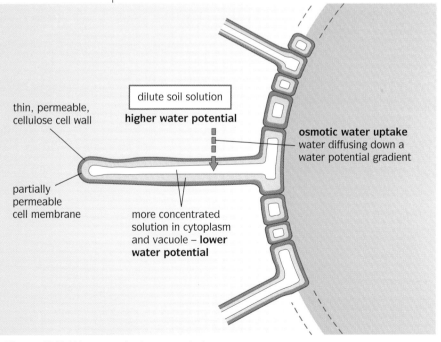

thin, permeable, cellulose cell wall

dilute soil solution
higher water potential

osmotic water uptake
water diffusing down a water potential gradient

partially permeable cell membrane

more concentrated solution in cytoplasm and vacuole – **lower water potential**

● *Figure 3.3* Water uptake by a root hair.

From root hair to xylem

Figures 3.4 and *3.5* show transverse sections of a young root. Water taken up by root hairs crosses the cortex and enters the xylem in the centre of the

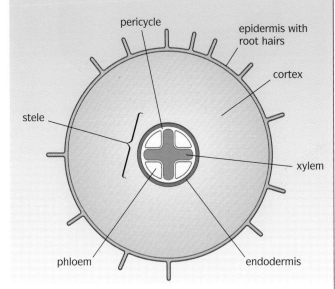

● *Figure 3.4* Transverse section of a young root to show the distribution of tissues.

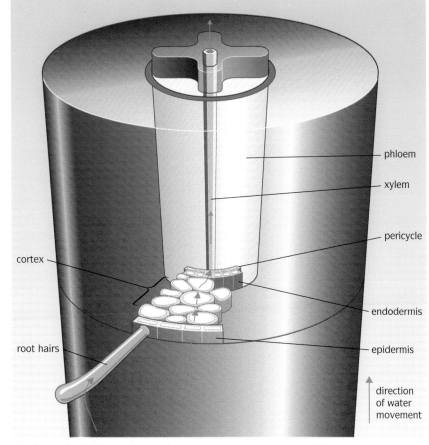

● *Figure 3.5* The pathway of water movement from root hair to xylem.

root. It does this because the water potential inside the xylem vessels, for reasons to be explained later, is lower than the water potential in the root hairs. Therefore, the water moves down this water potential gradient across the root.

The water can, and does, take two possible routes through the cortex (*figure 3.6*). The cells of the cortex, like all plant cells, are surrounded by cell walls made of several layers of cellulose fibres criss-crossing one another. Water can soak into these walls rather as it would soak into blotting paper, and can seep across the root from cell wall to cell wall without ever entering the cytoplasm of the cortical cells. This route is called the **apoplast pathway**. Another possibility is for the water to move into the cytoplasm or vacuole of a cortical cell, and then into adjacent cells through the interconnecting plasmodesmata. This is the **symplast pathway**. The relative importance of these two pathways varies from plant to plant, and in different conditions. Normally, it is probable that the symplast pathway is more important but, when transpiration rates (see page 37) are especially high, more water travels by the apoplast pathway.

Once the water reaches the stele, the apoplast pathway is abruptly barred. The cells in the outer layer surrounding the stele, the **endodermis**, have a thick, waterproof, waxy band of **suberin** in their cell walls (*figure 3.7*). This band, called the **Casparian strip**, forms an impenetrable barrier to water in the cell walls of the endodermis cells. The only way for the water to cross the endodermis is through the cytoplasm of these cells. As the endodermal cells get older, the suberin deposits become more extensive, except in certain cells called **passage cells**, through which water can pass.

Once across the endodermis, water continues to move down the water potential gradient across the pericycle and towards the xylem vessels.

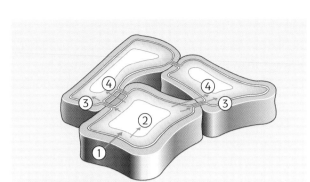

Symplast pathway

① Water enters the cytoplasm through the partially permeable cell membrane.

② Water moves into the sap in the vacuole, through the tonoplast.

③ Water may move from cell to cell through the plasmodesmata.

④ Water may move from cell to cell through adjacent cell surface membranes and cell walls.

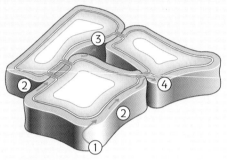

Apoplast pathway

① Water enters the cell wall.

② Water moves through the cell wall.

③ Water moves from cell wall to cell wall, through the intercellular spaces.

④ Water moves directly from cell wall to cell wall.

● **Figure 3.6** Apoplast and symplast pathways.

Xylem tissue

A tissue is a group of cells working together to perform a particular function. Xylem tissue *(figure 3.8)* has the dual functions of support and transport. The cells contained in xylem tissue include sclerenchyma and vessel elements. Sclerenchyma cells have thickened walls and help to support the plant. They are not involved in transport, so only vessels will be considered here.

Figure 3.9 shows the structure of a typical xylem vessel. Vessels are made up of many elongated **vessel elements** arranged end to end. Each began

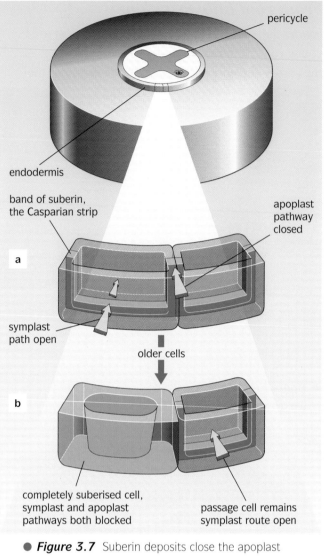

● **Figure 3.7** Suberin deposits close the apoplast pathway for water in the endodermis.

a In a young root the suberin deposits form bands in the cell walls called Casparian strips.

b In an older root, entire cells become suberised, leaving only certain passage cells permeable to water.

life as a normal plant cell in whose wall a substance called **lignin** was laid down. Lignin is a very hard, strong substance, which is impermeable to water. As it built up around the cell, the contents of the cell died, leaving a completely empty space, or **lumen**, inside. However, in several parts of the original cell walls, where groups of plasmodesmata were, no lignin was laid down. These non-lignified areas can be seen as 'gaps' in the thick walls of the xylem vessel, and are called **pits**. Pits are not open pores; they are crossed by permeable, unthickened cellulose cell wall.

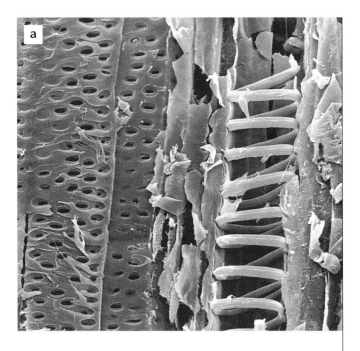

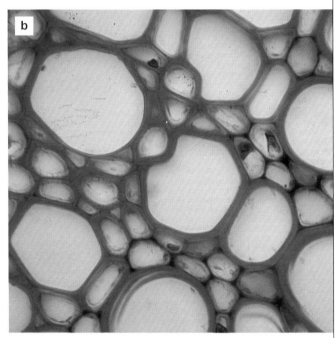

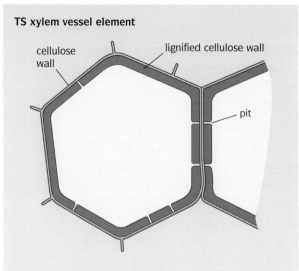

TS xylem vessel element

cellulose wall

lignified cellulose wall

pit

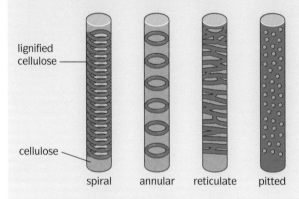

Types of lignified cell wall thickenings

lignified cellulose

cellulose

spiral   annular   reticulate   pitted

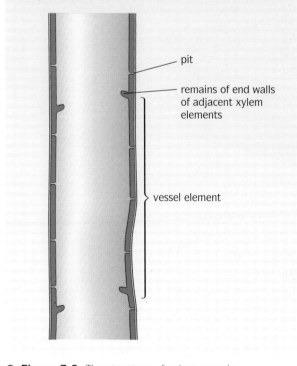

LS xylem vessel

pit

remains of end walls of adjacent xylem elements

vessel element

● *Figure 3.8* Xylem tissue.

a Scanning electron micrograph of a longitudinal section through part of a buttercup stem, showing xylem vessels. The young vessel on the right has a spiral band of lignin around it, while those on the left are older and have more extensive coverings of lignin with many pits.

b Light micrograph of a transverse section of xylem vessels. They have been stained so that the lignin appears red. The xylem vessels are the large empty cells. You can also see smaller parenchyma cells between them; these do not have lignified walls, and contain nucleus and cytoplasm.

● *Figure 3.9* The structure of xylem vessels.

The end walls of neighbouring vessel elements break down completely, to form a continuous tube rather like a drainpipe running through the plant. This long, non-living tube is a **xylem vessel**.

In the root, water which has crossed the cortex, endodermis and pericycle moves into the xylem vessels through the pits in their walls. It then moves up the vessels towards the leaves. Whereas the xylem vessels are in the centre of the root, in the stem they are nearer to the outside *(figure 3.10)*.

What causes water to move up xylem vessels? In order to explain this, we must look at what happens to water in a plant's leaves.

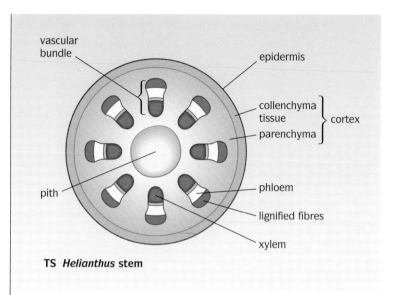

TS *Helianthus* stem

● *Figure 3.10* Transverse section of a young stem to show the distribution of tissues.

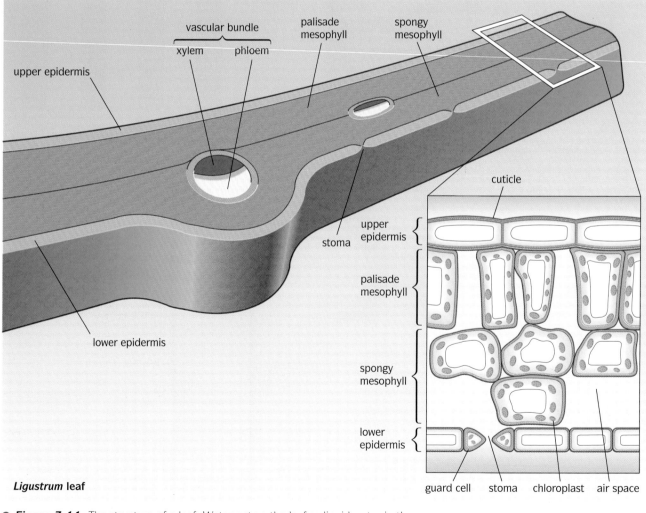

Ligustrum leaf

● *Figure 3.11* The structure of a leaf. Water enters the leaf as liquid water in the xylem vessels, and diffuses out as water vapour through the stomata.

Transpiration

Figure 3.11 shows the internal structure of a leaf. The cells in the **mesophyll** ('middle leaf') layers are not tightly packed, and have many spaces around them filled with air. The cell walls of the mesophyll cells are wet. Some of the water from the cell walls evaporates into the air spaces (*figure 3.12*), so that the air inside the leaf is usually saturated with water vapour.

The air in the internal spaces of the leaf has direct contact with the air outside the leaf, through small pores or **stomata**. If there is a water potential gradient between the air inside the leaf and the air outside, then water vapour will diffuse out of the leaf down this gradient. This loss of water vapour from the leaves of a plant is called **transpiration**.

An increase in the water potential gradient between the air spaces in the leaf and the air outside will increase the rate of transpiration. In conditions of low humidity, the gradient is steep, so transpiration takes place more quickly than in high humidity. Transpiration may also be increased by an increase in wind speed or a rise in temperature.

SAQ 3.1

Suggest how **a** an increase in wind speed, and **b** a rise in temperature, may cause the rate of transpiration to increase.

Another factor which affects the rate of transpiration is the opening or closing of the stomata. The stomata are the means of contact between photosynthesising mesophyll cells and the external air, and must be open to allow carbon dioxide for photosynthesis to diffuse into the leaf. On a bright, sunny day, when the rate of photosynthesis is likely to be high, then demand for carbon dioxide by the mesophyll cells means that stomata must be open. This inevitably increases the rate of transpiration.

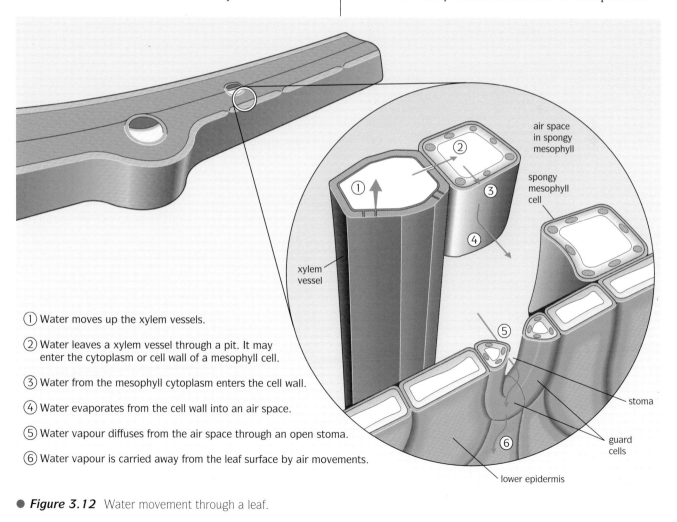

① Water moves up the xylem vessels.

② Water leaves a xylem vessel through a pit. It may enter the cytoplasm or cell wall of a mesophyll cell.

③ Water from the mesophyll cytoplasm enters the cell wall.

④ Water evaporates from the cell wall into an air space.

⑤ Water vapour diffuses from the air space through an open stoma.

⑥ Water vapour is carried away from the leaf surface by air movements.

● **Figure 3.12** Water movement through a leaf.

In especially dry conditions, when the water potential gradient between the internal air spaces and the external air is steep, a plant may have to compromise by partially closing its stomata to prevent its leaves drying out, even if this means reducing the rate of photosynthesis.

In hot conditions, transpiration can be important in cooling leaves. As water evaporates from the cell walls inside the leaf, it absorbs heat energy from these cells (latent heat of evaporation), thus reducing their temperature.

SAQ 3.2

How does this cooling mechanism compare with the main cooling mechanism of mammals?

● **Figure 3.13** If the rate at which water vapour is lost by transpiration exceeds the rate at which a plant can take up water from the soil, then the amount of water in its cells decreases. The cells lose turgor and the plant wilts as the soft parts, such as leaves, lose the support provided by turgid cells. Wilting actually helps the plant to reduce further water loss, because it reduces the surface area of the leaves in contact with the air, and so decreases the rate at which water vapour diffuses out of the leaves. In this situation the plant will also close its stomata.

Why water moves up xylem vessels

The amount of water vapour lost by transpiration from the leaves of a plant can be very great. Even in the relatively cool and moist conditions of a temperate country such as Britain, a leaf may lose the volume of water contained in its leaves every 20 minutes. Thus water must move into the leaves equally rapidly to replace this lost water.

As water evaporates from the cell walls of mesophyll cells, more water is drawn into them to replace it. The source of this water is the **xylem vessels** in the leaf. Water constantly moves out of these vessels, down a water potential gradient, either into the mesophyll cells or along their cell walls. Some will be used in photosynthesis, but most eventually evaporates and then diffuses out of the leaf.

The removal of water from the top of xylem vessels reduces the hydrostatic pressure. (Hydrostatic pressure is pressure exerted by a liquid.) The hydrostatic pressure at the top of the xylem vessel becomes lower than the pressure at the bottom. This pressure difference causes water to move up the xylem vessels. It is just like sucking water up a straw. Your 'suck' at the top reduces the pressure at the top of the straw, causing a pressure difference between the top and bottom which pushes water up the straw.

The water in the xylem vessels, like the liquid in a 'sucked' straw, is under tension. If you suck hard on a straw, its walls may collapse inwards as a result of the pressure differences you are creating. Xylem vessels have strong, lignified walls to stop them from collapsing in this way.

The movement of water up through xylem vessels is by **mass flow**. This means that all the water molecules move together, as a body of liquid. This is helped by the fact that water molecules are attracted to each other, the attraction being called **cohesion**. They are also attracted to the lignin in the walls of the xylem vessels, this attraction being called **adhesion**. Cohesion and adhesion help to keep the water in a xylem vessel moving as a continuous column.

If an air bubble forms in the column, then the column of water breaks and the difference in pressure between the water at the top and the water at the bottom cannot be transmitted through the vessel. We say there is an *air lock*. The water stops moving upwards. The small diameter of xylem vessels helps to prevent such breaks from occurring. The pits in the vessel walls also allow water to move out, which may allow it to move from one vessel to another and so bypass such an air lock. Air bubbles cannot pass through pits. Pits are also important in allowing water to move out of xylem vessels to surrounding living cells.

Root pressure

You have seen how transpiration *reduces* the water pressure at the top of a xylem vessel compared with the pressure at the base, so causing the water to flow up the vessels. Plants may also increase the pressure difference between the top and bottom by *raising* the water pressure at the base of the vessels.

The pressure is raised by the active secretion of solutes, for example mineral ions, into the water in the xylem vessels in the root. Cells surrounding the xylem vessels use energy to push solutes across their membranes and into the xylem by active transport. The presence of the solutes lowers the water potential of the solution in the xylem, thus drawing in water from the surrounding root cells. This influx of water increases the water pressure at the base of the xylem vessel.

Although root pressure may help in moving water up xylem vessels, it is not essential, and is probably not significant in causing water to move up xylem in most plants. Water can continue to move up through xylem even if the plant is dead. Water transport in plants is largely a **passive** process, fuelled by transpiration from the leaves. The water simply moves down a continuous water potential gradient from the soil to the air.

SAQ 3.3

Transport of water from the environment to cells occurs in both plants and mammals. For both plants and mammals, state the stages of this transport in which water moves by

a osmosis, and   **b** mass flow.

SAQ 3.4

Explain how each of the following features of xylem vessels adapts them for their function of transporting water from roots to leaves.

a Total lack of cell contents
b No end walls in individual xylem elements
c A diameter of between 0.01 mm and 0.2 mm
d Lignified walls
e Pits

Translocation

Translocation is the term used to describe the transport of soluble organic substances within a plant. These are substances which the plant itself has made, for example sugars which are made by photosynthesis in the leaves. These substances are sometimes called **assimilates**.

Assimilates are transported in **sieve tubes**. Sieve tubes are found in **phloem tissue**, along with several other types of cells including **companion cells** (figure 3.14).

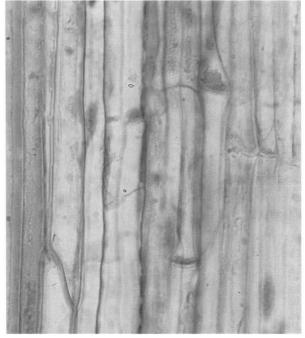

● *Figure 3.14* Light micrograph of a longitudinal section through phloem tissue. The places where the tubes widen, looking almost like a joint, are the sieve plates. Notice how thin the walls of the phloem sieve tubes are compared with those of the xylem vessels in *figure 3.8*, and also that these cells contain cytoplasm, in contrast to the completely empty xylem vessels.

Sieve elements

Figure 3.15 shows the structure of a sieve tube and its accompanying companion cells. A sieve tube is made up many elongated **sieve elements**, joined end to end vertically to form a continuous column. Each sieve element is a living cell. Like a 'normal' plant cell, it has a cellulose cell wall, a cell membrane and cytoplasm containing endoplasmic reticulum and mitochondria. However, the amount of cytoplasm is very small and only forms a thin layer lining the inside of the wall of the cell. There is no nucleus, nor are there any ribosomes.

Perhaps the most striking feature of sieve elements is their end walls. Where the end walls of two sieve elements meet, a **sieve plate** is formed. This is made up of the walls of both elements, through which large pores pass. These pores are easily visible with a good light microscope. When sieve plates are viewed using an electron microscope, strands of fibrous protein can sometimes be seen passing through these pores from one sieve element to another. However, these strands have been produced by the sieve element in response to the damage caused when the tissue is cut during preparation of the specimen for viewing. In living phloem the protein strands are not present; the pores are open, presenting little barrier to the free flow of liquids through them.

Companion cells

Each sieve element has at least one companion cell lying close beside it. Companion cells have the structure of a 'normal' plant cell, with a cellulose cell wall, a cell membrane, cytoplasm, a small vacuole and a nucleus. However, the number of

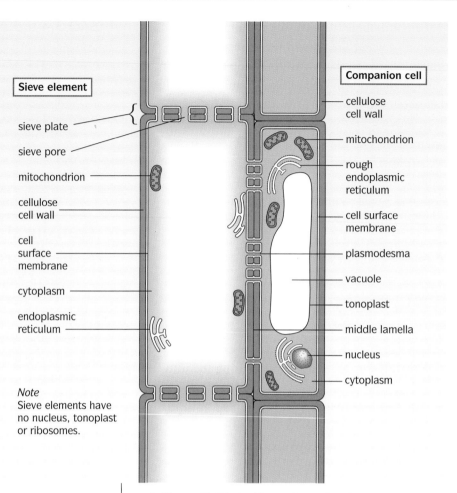

Sieve element
- sieve plate
- sieve pore
- mitochondrion
- cellulose cell wall
- cell surface membrane
- cytoplasm
- endoplasmic reticulum

Note
Sieve elements have no nucleus, tonoplast or ribosomes.

Companion cell
- cellulose cell wall
- mitochondrion
- rough endoplasmic reticulum
- cell surface membrane
- plasmodesma
- vacuole
- tonoplast
- middle lamella
- nucleus
- cytoplasm

● *Figure 3.15* A phloem sieve tube element and its companion cell.

mitochondria and ribosomes is rather larger than normal, and the cells are metabolically very active.

Companion cells are very closely associated with their neighbouring sieve elements. Numerous plasmodesmata pass through their cell walls, making direct contact between the cytoplasm of the companion cell and sieve element.

The contents of phloem sieve tubes

The liquid inside phloem sieve tubes is called **phloem sap**, or just sap. *Table 3.1* shows the composition of the sap of the castor oil plant, *Ricinus communis*.

SAQ 3.5

Which of the substances listed in *table 3.1* have been synthesised by the plant?

Solute	Concentration/mol m^{-3}
sucrose	250
potassium ions	80
amino acids	40
chloride ions	15
phosphate ions	10
magnesium ions	5
sodium ions	2
ATP	0.5
nitrate ions	0
plant growth substances (e.g. auxin, cytokinin)	small traces

● **Table 3.1**

It is not easy to collect enough phloem sap to analyse its contents. When phloem tissue is cut, the sieve elements respond by rapidly blocking the sieve pores, in a process sometimes called 'clotting'. The pores are blocked first by plugs of phloem protein and then, within hours, by the carbohydrate **callose**. (Callose has a molecular structure very similar to cellulose. Like cellulose, its molecules are long chains of glucose units, but these are linked by β 1,3 glycosidic bonds, rather than the β 1,4 bonds of cellulose.) However, castor oil plants are unusual in that their phloem sap does continue to flow from a cut for some time, making it relatively easy to collect.

In other plants, aphids may be used to sample sap. Aphids, such as greenfly, feed using tubular mouthparts called stylets. They insert these through the surface of the plant's stem or leaves, into the phloem *(figure 3.16)*. Phloem sap flows through the stylet into the aphid. If the stylet is cut near the aphid's head, the sap continues to flow; it seems that the small diameter of the stylet does not allow sap to flow out rapidly enough to switch on the plant's phloem 'clotting' mechanism.

How translocation occurs

Phloem sap, like the contents of xylem vessels, moves by **mass flow**. However, whereas in xylem vessels differences in pressure are produced by a water potential gradient between soil and air, requiring no energy input from the plant, this is not so in phloem transport. To create the pressure differences needed for mass flow in phloem, the plant has to use energy. Phloem transport can therefore be considered an **active** process, in contrast to the **passive** transport in xylem.

The pressure difference is produced by **active loading** of sucrose into the sieve elements at the place from which sucrose is to be transported. This is usually in a photosynthesising leaf. As sucrose is loaded into the sieve element, this decreases the water potential in the sap inside it. Therefore, water follows the sucrose into the sieve element, moving down a water potential gradient by osmosis.

At another point along the sieve tube, sucrose may be removed by other cells, for example in the root. As sucrose is removed, water again follows by osmosis.

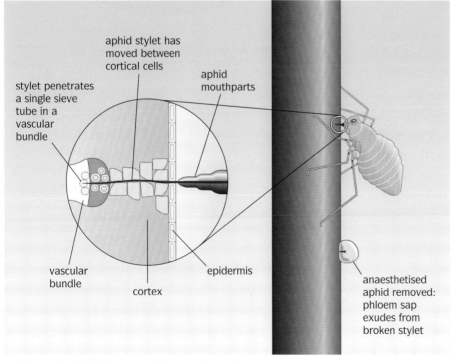

● **Figure 3.16** Using an aphid to collect phloem sap.

stylet penetrates a single sieve tube in a vascular bundle

aphid stylet has moved between cortical cells

aphid mouthparts

vascular bundle

cortex

epidermis

anaesthetised aphid removed: phloem sap exudes from broken stylet

● **Figure 3.17** The phloem sap of the sugar maple contains a high concentration of sugar, and in some parts of North America it is harvested to make maple syrup, A tap is inserted into the tree to allow the sap to run out under its own pressure.

Thus, in the leaf, water moves into the sieve tube. In the root, water moves out of it. This creates a pressure difference; hydrostatic pressure is high in the part of the sieve tube in the leaf, and lower in the part in the root *(figure 3.18)*. This pressure difference causes water to flow from the high pressure area to the low pressure area, taking with it any solutes.

Sources and sinks

Any area of a plant in which sucrose is loaded into the phloem is called a **source**. Usually, the source is a photosynthesising leaf. Any area where sucrose is taken out of the phloem is called a **sink**.

SAQ 3.6

Which of the following will be sources, and which will be sinks?
A nectary in a flower
A developing fruit
The storage tissue of a potato tuber when the buds are beginning to sprout
A developing potato tuber

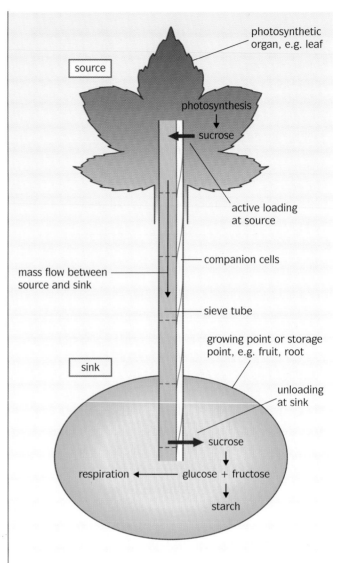

● **Figure 3.18** Sources, sinks and mass flow in phloem.

Sinks can be anywhere in the plant, both above and below the photosynthesising leaves. Thus, sap flows both upwards and downwards in phloem (in contrast with xylem, in which flow is always upwards). Within any vascular bundle, phloem sap may be flowing upwards in some sieve tubes and downwards in others, but it can only flow one way in any particular sieve tube at any one time.

Loading of sucrose into phloem

In leaf mesophyll cells, photosynthesis in chloroplasts produces **triose phosphate**. This moves out of the chloroplast into the cytoplasm where the enzyme **sucrose phosphate synthetase** converts it into sucrose.

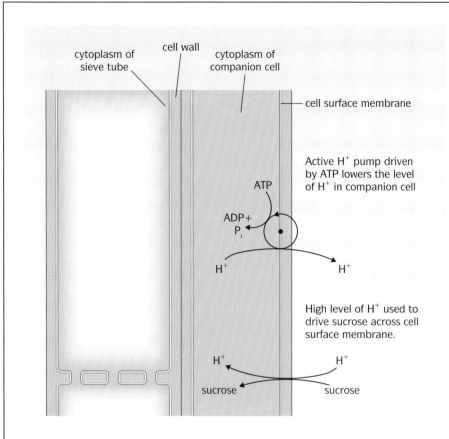

cytoplasm of
sieve tube

cell wall

cytoplasm of
companion cell

cell surface membrane

Active H⁺ pump driven
by ATP lowers the level
of H⁺ in companion cell

ATP

ADP+
P$_i$

H⁺

H⁺

High level of H⁺ used to
drive sucrose across cell
surface membrane.

H⁺

sucrose

H⁺

sucrose

● *Figure 3.19* A possible method by which sucrose is loaded into phloem.

The sucrose, in solution, then moves from the mesophyll cell, across the leaf to the phloem tissue. It may move by the symplast pathway, moving from cell to cell via plasmodesmata. Alternatively, it may move by the apoplast pathway, travelling along cell walls. Which of these routes is more important varies between species.

Sucrose is loaded into a companion cell by active transport. *Figure 3.19* shows how this may be done. Hydrogen ions are moved out of the companion cell, using ATP as an energy source. This creates a large excess of hydrogen ions outside the companion cell. They can move back into the cell down their concentration gradient, through a protein which acts as a carrier for both hydrogen ions and sucrose at the same time. The sucrose

molecules are carried through this co-transporter molecule into the companion cell, against the concentration gradient for sucrose. The sucrose molecules can then move from the companion cell into the sieve tube, through the plasmodesmata which connect them.

Unloading of sucrose from phloem

At the moment, little is known about the way in which sucrose is unloaded from phloem. Unloading occurs into any tissue which requires sucrose. It is probable that sucrose moves out of the phloem into these tissues by diffusion. Once in the tissue, the sucrose is converted into something else by enzymes, so decreasing its concentration and maintaining a concentration gradient. One such enzyme is invertase, which hydrolyses sucrose to glucose and fructose.

Evidence for the mechanism of phloem transport

Until the late 1970s and early 1980s, there was considerable argument about whether or not phloem sap did or did not move by mass flow, in the way described above. The stumbling block was the presence of the sieve pores and phloem protein, as it was felt that these must have some important role. Several hypotheses were put forward which tried to provide a role for the phloem protein, and you may come across some of these in various textbooks. It is now known that phloem protein is not present in living, active phloem tissue, and so there is no need to provide it with a role when explaining the mechanism of phloem transport.

The evidence that phloem transport does occur by mass flow is considerable. The rate of transport in phloem is about 10 000 times faster than it would be if substances were moving by diffusion rather than by mass flow. The actual rates of transport measured match closely with those calculated from measured pressure differences at source and sink, assuming that the pores in the sieve plates are open and unobstructed.

There is also considerable evidence for the active loading of sucrose into sieve elements in sources such as leaves. Much experimental work has been done in investigating the sucrose–hydrogen ion cotransporter system in plant cells, although it has so far been very difficult to investigate this in companion cells and phloem sieve elements. Nevertheless, there is much circumstantial evidence that active loading of sucrose into phloem sieve tubes, as described above, does take place. This includes the following observations.

■ Phloem sap always has a relatively high pH, often around 8. This is what would be expected if hydrogen ions were being actively transported out of the cell.

■ There is a difference in electrical potential across the cell surface membrane of around $-150\,mV$ inside, again consistent with an excess of positive hydrogen ions outside the cell compared with inside.

■ ATP is present in phloem sieve elements in quite large amounts. This would be expected, as it is required for the active transport of hydrogen ions out of the cell.

Differences between sieve elements and xylem vessels

From this account of translocation, several similarities with the transport of water emerge. In each case, liquid moves by mass flow along a pressure gradient, through tubes formed by cells stacked end to end. So why are phloem sieve tubes so different in structure from xylem vessels?

Unlike water transport through xylem, which occurs through dead xylem vessels, translocation through phloem sieve tubes involves active loading of sucrose at sources, thus requiring living cells.

Xylem vessels have lignified cell walls, whereas phloem tubes do not. The presence of lignin in a cell wall prevents the movement of water and solutes across it, and so kills the cell. This does not matter in xylem, as xylem does not need to be alive; indeed, it is a positive advantage to have an entirely empty tube through which water can flow unimpeded, and the dead xylem vessels with their strong walls also support the plant. Sieve tubes, however, must remain alive, and so no lignin is deposited in their cellulose cell walls.

The end walls of xylem elements disappear completely, whereas those of phloem sieve elements form sieve plates. These sieve plates probably act as supporting structures to prevent the phloem sieve tube collapsing; xylem already has sufficient support provided by its lignified walls. The sieve plates also allow the phloem to seal itself up rapidly if damaged, for example by a grazing herbivore, rather as a blood vessel in an animal is sealed by clotting. Phloem sap has a high turgor pressure because of its high solute content, and would leak out rapidly if the holes in the sieve plate were not quickly sealed. Moreover, phloem sap contains valuable substances such as sucrose, which the plant cannot afford to lose in large quantity. The 'clotting' of phloem sap may also help to prevent the entry of microorganisms which might feed on the nutritious sap or cause disease.

SAQ 3.7

Draw up a comparison table between xylem vessels and sieve tubes. Some features which you could include are: cell structure (walls, diameter, cell contents, etc.), substances transported and methods of transport. Include a column giving a brief explanation for the differences in structure.

SUMMARY

■ Water is transported through a plant in xylem vessels. This is a passive process, in which water moves down a water potential gradient from soil to air. Water enters root hairs by osmosis, crosses the root either through the cytoplasm of cells or via their cell walls, and enters the dead, empty xylem vessels. Water moves up xylem vessels by mass flow, as a result of pressure differences caused by loss of water from leaves by transpiration. Root pressure may contribute to this pressure difference.

■ Transpiration is an inevitable consequence of gas exchange in plants. Plants have air spaces within the leaf in communication with the external atmosphere through stomata, so that carbon dioxide and oxygen can be exchanged with their environment. Water vapour, formed as water evaporates from wet cell walls, also diffuses through these air spaces and out of the stomata.

■ Translocation of organic solutes, such as sucrose, occurs through living phloem sieve tubes. The phloem sap moves by mass flow, as a result of pressure differences produced by active loading of sucrose at sources such as photosynthesising leaves.

Questions

1 Discuss the similarities and differences between the transport systems of plants and mammals.

2 Describe the pathway and mechanisms by which water travels through a plant, from the soil into the atmosphere.

3 Construct a table to compare and contrast the mechanisms of transport in the xylem and phloem.

4 Plants which live in environments where the soil water is very salty, such as estuaries, are called halophytes.

   a What problems might halophytes have to overcome with regard to taking up water and maintaining a suitable salt and water concentration in their cells?

   b Suggest how each of the following adaptations might help a halophyte to overcome these problems.

   • Rapid active uptake of ions, such as Na^+ and Cl^-, by the roots.

   • Ability to tolerate low water potentials in cell sap and cytoplasm.

   • Ability to maintain higher salt concentrations in cell vacuoles than in cytoplasm, by active transport of Na^+ and Cl^- across the tonoplast.

   • Salt glands in leaves, which actively excrete salt onto the surface of the leaf.

Excretion

Many of the metabolic reactions occurring within the body produce unwanted substances. Some of these are toxic (poisonous). The removal of these unwanted products of metabolism is known as **excretion.**

Many excretory products are formed in humans, but three are made in much greater amounts than the others. These are **carbon dioxide, urea** and **bilirubin.**

Carbon dioxide is produced virtually continuously by almost every cell in the body, by the reactions of aerobic respiration. The waste carbon dioxide is transported from the respiring cells to the lungs, in the bloodstream (page 17). It diffuses from the blood into the alveoli of the lungs, and is excreted in the air we breathe out.

In contrast, urea is produced in only one organ in the body, that is the **liver.** It is produced from excess amino acids (as described in

the next section) and is transported from the liver to the kidneys, in solution in blood plasma. The kidneys remove urea from the blood and excrete it, dissolved in water, as urine.

Bilirubin is also made in the liver, from the haemoglobin in old red blood cells. It is excreted in bile. This is described more fully in chapter 6.

Here, we will look more fully at the production and excretion of urea.

Deamination

If more protein is eaten than is needed, the excess cannot be stored in the body. It would be wasteful, however, simply to get rid of all the excess, because the amino acids contain useful energy. The liver salvages this energy by removing the nitrogen atoms from the amino acids, excreting these in the form of urea, and keeping the rest of each amino acid molecule. The process by which urea is made from excess amino acids is called **deamination.**

Figure 4.1 shows how deamination takes place. In the liver cells, the amino (NH_2) group of an amino acid is removed, together with an extra hydrogen atom. These combine to produce ammonia. The keto acid that remains may become a carbohydrate, which can be used in respiration, or may be converted to fat and stored.

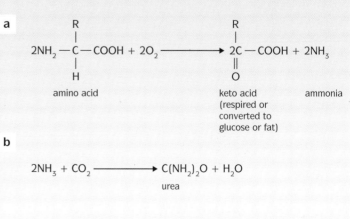

● **Figure 4.1** **a** Deamination.   **b** Urea formation.

Ammonia is a very soluble and highly toxic compound. In aquatic animals, such as fish, this poses no danger as the ammonia can simply dissolve into the water around them. However, in terrestrial animals, such as humans, ammonia would rapidly build up in the blood and cause immense damage. So the ammonia produced in the liver is instantly converted to the less soluble and less toxic compound, **urea**. Urea is made by combining ammonia with carbon dioxide. An adult produces around 25–30g of urea per day.

Urea is the main **nitrogenous excretory product** of humans. We also produce small quantities of other nitrogenous excretory products, mainly **creatinine** and **uric acid**. Creatine is made in the liver, from certain amino acids. Much of this creatine is used in the muscles, in the form of creatine phosphate, where it acts as an energy store. However, some is converted to creatinine and excreted. Uric acid is made from the break-down of nucleic acids, not from amino acids.

The urea made in the liver passes from the liver cells into the blood plasma. All of the urea made each day must be excreted, or its concentration in the blood would build up and become dangerous. As the blood passes through the kidneys, the urea is extracted and excreted. To explain how this happens, we must first look at the structure of a kidney.

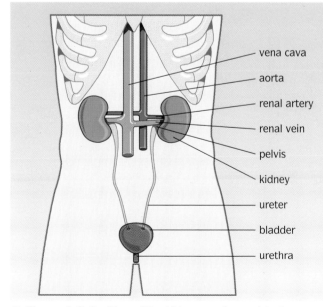

● *Figure 4.2* Position of the kidneys and associated structures in the human body.

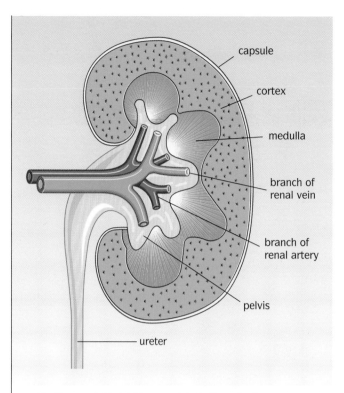

● *Figure 4.3* A kidney, cut in half vertically.

The structure of the kidney

Figure 4.2 shows the position of the kidneys in the body together with their associated structures. Each kidney receives blood from a **renal artery**, and returns blood via a **renal vein**. A narrow tube, called the **ureter**, carries urine from the kidney to the bladder. From there a single tube, the **urethra**, carries urine to the outside of the body.

A longitudinal section through a kidney (*figure 4.3*) shows that it has three main areas. The whole kidney is covered by a fairly tough **capsule**, beneath which lies the **cortex**. The central area is made up of the **medulla**. Where the ureter joins, there is an area called the **pelvis**.

A section through a kidney, seen through a microscope (*figure 4.5*), shows it to be made up of thousands of tiny tubes that are called **nephrons**. *Figure 4.4* shows the position and structure of a single nephron. One end of the tube forms a cup-shaped structure called a **renal (Bowman's) capsule**. The renal capsules of all nephrons are in the cortex of the kidney. From the renal capsule, the tube runs towards the centre of the kidney, first

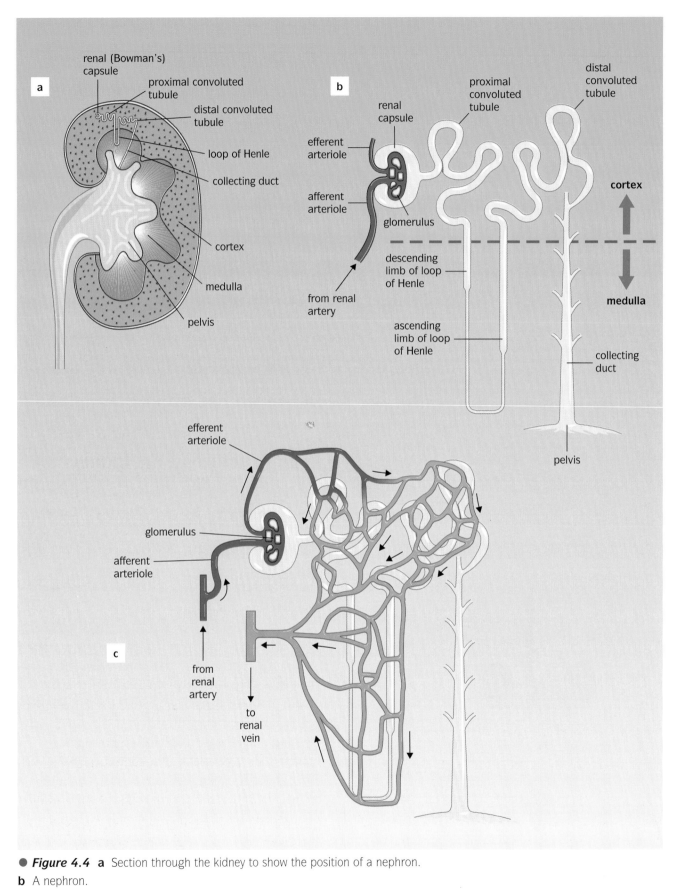

● *Figure 4.4* **a** Section through the kidney to show the position of a nephron.
b A nephron.
c The blood supply associated with a nephron.

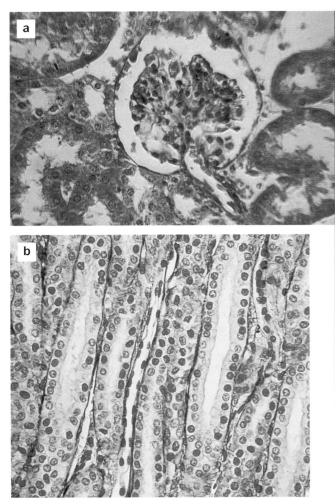

a

b

● *Figure 4.5*

a Light micrograph of a section through the cortex of a kidney. The white circular area in the centre is the lumen of a renal capsule. You can pick out the beginning of the proximal convoluted tubule leading downwards from it. The darkly stained area in the centre of the capsule contains the blood capillaries of the glomerulus. There are also several proximal convoluted tubules and distal convoluted tubules in transverse section.

b Light micrograph of a longitudinal section through the medulla of a kidney. This section cuts through several loops of Henle (relatively narrow) and collecting ducts (relatively wide, with almost cubical cells making up their walls). You can also see some blood capillaries.

forming a twisted region called the **proximal convoluted tubule**, and then a long hairpin loop in the medulla, the **loop of Henle**. The tubule then runs back upwards into the cortex, where it forms another twisted region called the **distal convoluted tubule**, before finally joining a **collecting duct**

which leads down through the medulla and into the pelvis of the kidney. Here the collecting ducts join the ureter.

Blood vessels are closely associated with the nephrons *(figure 4.4c)*. Each renal capsule is supplied with blood by a branch of the renal artery, called an **afferent arteriole**, which splits into a tangle of capillaries in the 'cup' of the capsule, called a **glomerulus**. The capillaries of the glomerulus rejoin to form an **efferent arteriole**. This leads off to form a network of capillaries running closely alongside the rest of the nephron, before linking up with other capillaries to feed into a branch of the renal vein.

Ultrafiltration

The kidney makes urine in a two-stage process. The first stage, **ultrafiltration**, involves filtering small molecules, including urea, out of the blood and into the renal capsule. From here they flow along the nephron towards the ureter. The second stage, **reabsorption**, involves taking back any useful molecules from the fluid in the nephron as it flows along.

Figure 4.6 shows a section through part of a glomerulus and renal capsule. The blood in the glomerular capillaries is separated from the lumen of the renal capsule by two cell layers and a basement membrane. The first cell layer is the lining, or **endothelium**, of the capillary. Like the endothelium of most capillaries, this has gaps in it, but there are far more gaps than in other capillaries: each endothelial cell has thousands of tiny holes in it. Next comes the **basement membrane** which is made up of a network of collagen and glycoproteins. The second cell layer is formed from **epithelial cells** which make up the wall of the renal capsule. These cells have many tiny finger-like projections, with gaps in between them. The cells are called **podocytes**.

The holes in the capillary endothelium, and the gaps in the renal capsule epithelium, are quite large, and make it easy for any substances dissolved in the blood plasma to get through from the blood into the capsule. However, the basement membrane stops large protein molecules from

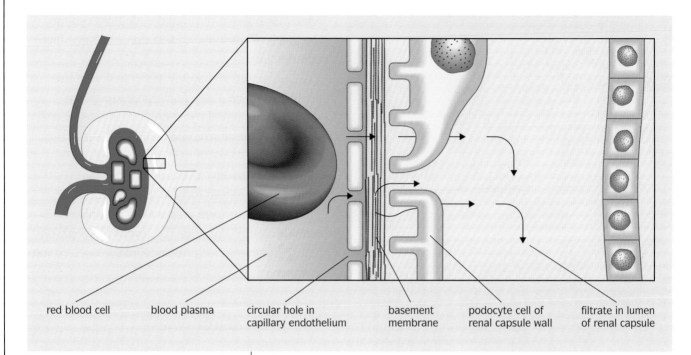

red blood cell   blood plasma   circular hole in capillary endothelium   basement membrane   podocyte cell of renal capsule wall   filtrate in lumen of renal capsule

● **Figure 4.6** Detail of the wall of a glomerular capillary and renal capsule, showing how ultrafiltration occurs. The arrows show how fluid moves out of the capillary and into the lumen of the capsule. The basement membrane acts as a molecular filter.

getting through. Any protein molecule with a relative molecular mass of around 69 000 or more cannot pass through the basement membrane, and so cannot escape from the glomerular capillaries. This basement membrane therefore acts as a filter. Blood cells, both red and white, are also too large to pass through this barrier, and so remain in the blood. *Table 4.1* shows the relative concentrations of substances in the blood and in the glomerular filtrate. You will see that glomerular filtrate is identical to blood plasma minus plasma proteins.

Factors affecting glomerular filtration rate

The rate at which fluid seeps from the blood in the glomerular capillaries, into the renal capsule, is called the **glomerular filtration rate**. In a human, for all the glomeruli in both kidneys, this is about $125 \, cm^3 \, min^{-1}$.

What makes the fluid filter through so quickly? The main force pushing it through is the relatively high **hydrostatic pressure** in the glomerular capillaries. This is produced because the afferent arteriole has a wider diameter than the efferent arteriole, so causing a 'traffic jam' in the glomerulus which builds up blood pressure. In humans, an average value for this pressure is about 7.8 kPa. The pressure inside the renal capsule is considerably lower, around 2.3 kPa. Thus, the net hydrostatic pressure pushing fluid from the capillaries into the renal capsule is $7.8 - 2.3 = 5.5 \, kPa$ *(figure 4.7)*.

Substance	Concentration in blood plasma/g dm^{-3}	Concentration in glomerular filtrate/g dm^{-3}
water	900.0	900.0
proteins	80.0	0.05
amino acids	0.5	0.5
glucose	1.0	1.0
urea	0.3	0.3
uric acid	0.04	0.04
creatinine	0.01	0.01
inorganic ions, mainly Na$^+$, K$^+$ and Cl$^-$	7.2	7.2

● **Table 4.1**

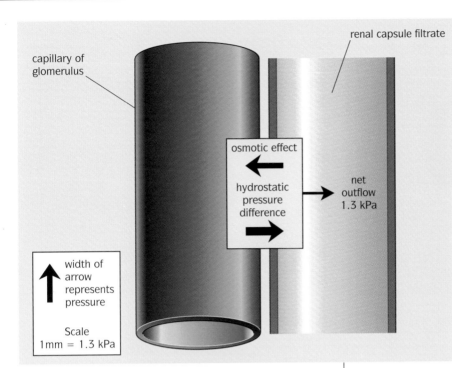

capillary of glomerulus

renal capsule filtrate

osmotic effect

hydrostatic pressure difference

net outflow 1.3 kPa

width of arrow represents pressure

Scale
1mm = 1.3 kPa

● *Figure 4.7* Hydrostatic pressure tends to force fluid from the glomerular capillaries into the renal capsule, while colloid osmotic pressure tends to push it the other way. The difference between the two produces a net pressure of around 1.3 kPa, forcing fluid out of the glomerulus and into the lumen of the capsule.

Reabsorption in the proximal convoluted tubule

The fluid which has filtered through into the renal capsule is virtually identical to blood plasma, except that it does not contain large protein molecules. Many of the substances in the filtrate need to be kept in the body, so they are reabsorbed into the blood as the fluid passes along the nephron. Since only certain substances are reabsorbed, the process is called **selective reabsorption**. Most of the reabsorption takes place in the proximal convoluted tubule.

The basal membranes (the ones nearest the blood and furthest from the lumen) of the cells lining the proximal convoluted tubule actively transport sodium ions out of the cell *(figure 4.8)*. The sodium ions are carried away in the blood. This lowers the concentration of sodium ions inside the cell, so that they passively diffuse into it, down their concentration gradient, from the fluid in the lumen of the tubule. However, they do not just diffuse freely through the membrane; they can only enter through special transporter (carrier) proteins in the membrane. There are several different kinds of these, each of which transports something else, such as glucose, at the same time as the sodium. The concentration gradient for the sodium provides enough energy to pull in glucose molecules. Thus glucose is taken up by the cell, and into the blood.

All of the **glucose** in the glomerular filtrate is transported out of the proximal convoluted tubule and into the blood. Normally, no glucose is left in the tubule, so no glucose is present in urine. Similarly, **amino acids**, **vitamins**, and many **sodium** and **chloride ions** are actively reabsorbed here.

The uptake of these substances would decrease the solute concentration of the filtrate. However, **water** can (and does) move freely out of the filtrate, through the walls of the tubule and into

However, these hydrostatic pressures are not the only forces affecting the rate of filtration. Osmotic forces must also be taken into account. As the water and soluble substances pass out of the glomerular capillaries into the renal capsule, the blood becomes a more concentrated solution as most of the proteins are left behind in the blood. The fluid in the renal capsule, however, does *not* contain proteins, and is more dilute. Thus, water has a tendency to move, by osmosis, back from the renal capsule into the capillaries. The force causing this tendency is called **colloid osmotic pressure**. A typical value in a human kidney is about 4.2 kPa.

Overall, then, there is a force of about 5.5 kPa pushing the fluid out of the glomerulus into the renal capsule, and a net force of about 4.2 kPa pushing fluid out of the renal capsule into the glomerulus. A simple subtraction sum shows that the net force pushing fluid from the glomerulus into the capsule is about 1.3 kPa.

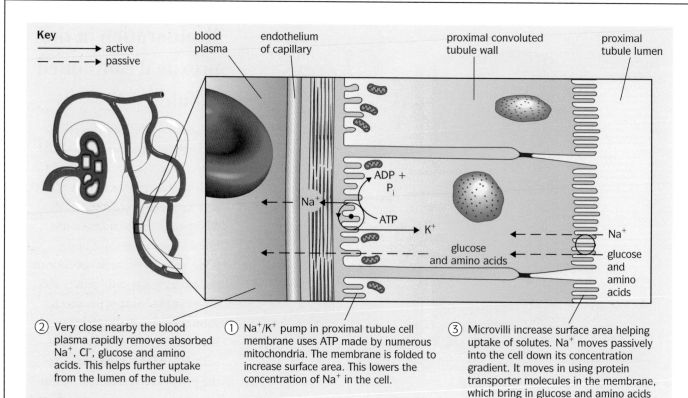

Key

→ active
- - - → passive

blood plasma

endothelium of capillary

proximal convoluted tubule wall

proximal tubule lumen

ADP + P$_i$

Na$^+$

ATP

K$^+$

glucose and amino acids

Na$^+$

glucose and amino acids

② Very close nearby the blood plasma rapidly removes absorbed Na$^+$, Cl$^-$, glucose and amino acids. This helps further uptake from the lumen of the tubule.

① Na$^+$/K$^+$ pump in proximal tubule cell membrane uses ATP made by numerous mitochondria. The membrane is folded to increase surface area. This lowers the concentration of Na$^+$ in the cell.

③ Microvilli increase surface area helping uptake of solutes. Na$^+$ moves passively into the cell down its concentration gradient. It moves in using protein transporter molecules in the membrane, which bring in glucose and amino acids at the same time.

● **Figure 4.8** Reabsorption in the proximal convoluted tubule.

the blood. As the substances listed above move into the cells surrounding the tubule, water follows by osmosis. Thus the overall concentration of the filtrate remains about the same. About 65% of the water in the filtrate is reabsorbed here.

SAQ 4.1

Look back at *figure 4.5*.

a Where has the blood in the capillaries surrounding the proximal convoluted tubule come from?

b What substances will this blood contain which are *not* present in the glomerular filtrate?

c How might this help in the reabsorption of water from the proximal convoluted tubule?

Surprisingly, quite a lot of urea is reabsorbed too. Urea is a small molecule, which passes easily through cell membranes. Its concentration in the glomerular filtrate is considerably higher than that in the capillaries, so it diffuses passively through the wall of the proximal convoluted tubule and into the blood. About half of the urea in the filtrate is reabsorbed in this way.

The other two nitrogenous excretory products,

uric acid and creatinine, are not reabsorbed. Indeed, creatinine is actively **secreted** by the cells of the proximal convoluted tubule into its lumen.

The reabsorption of so much water and solutes from the filtrate in the proximal convoluted tubule greatly reduces the volume of liquid remaining. In an adult human, around 125 cm^3 of fluid enter the proximal tubules every minute, but only 45 cm^3 per minute are passed on to the next region, the loop of Henle.

SAQ 4.2

Although almost half of the urea in the glomerular filtrate is reabsorbed from the proximal convoluted tubule, the *concentration* of urea in the fluid in the nephron actually increases as it passes through the proximal convoluted tubule. Explain why this is so.

Reabsorption in the loop of Henle and collecting duct

The function of the loop of Henle is to create a very high concentration of salts in the tissue fluid in the medulla of the kidney. As you will see, this allows a lot of water to be reabsorbed from the fluid in the collecting duct, as it flows through the medulla. As a result, very concentrated urine can be produced. The loop of Henle therefore allows water to be conserved in the body, rather than lost in urine.

Figure 4.9a shows the loop of Henle. The hairpin loop runs deep down into the medulla of the kidney, before turning back towards the cortex again. The first part of the loop is therefore called the **descending limb,** and the second part the **ascending limb.**

To explain how it works, it is best to begin by looking at what happens in the *second* part of the loop, the ascending limb. The walls of the upper parts of the loop are impermeable to water. The

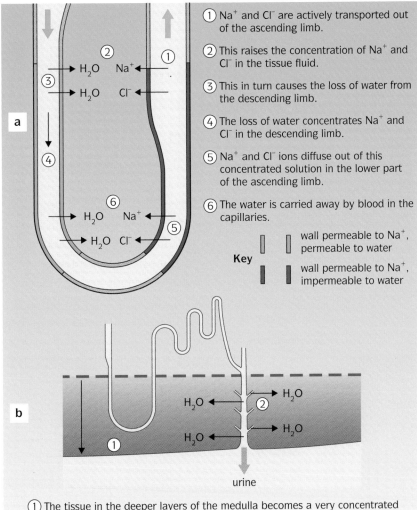

① Na⁺ and Cl⁻ are actively transported out of the ascending limb.

② This raises the concentration of Na⁺ and Cl⁻ in the tissue fluid.

③ This in turn causes the loss of water from the descending limb.

④ The loss of water concentrates Na⁺ and Cl⁻ in the descending limb.

⑤ Na⁺ and Cl⁻ ions diffuse out of this concentrated solution in the lower part of the ascending limb.

⑥ The water is carried away by blood in the capillaries.

Key
☐ wall permeable to Na⁺, permeable to water
▮ wall permeable to Na⁺, impermeable to water

① The tissue in the deeper layers of the medulla becomes a very concentrated solution of Na⁺, Cl⁻ and urea.

② As urine passes down the collecting duct, water can pass out of it by osmosis. The reabsorbed water is carried away by the blood in the capillaries.

● **Figure 4.9** How the loop of Henle allows the production of concentrated urine.
a The countercurrent mechanism in the loop of Henle builds up a high sodium ion and chloride ion concentration in the tissue fluid of the medulla.
b Water can be drawn out of the collecting duct by the high salt concentration in the surrounding tissue fluid.

cells in the walls of this area actively transport sodium and chloride ions out of the fluid in the tube, into the tissue fluid between the cells filling the space beween the two limbs. This produces a high concentration of sodium and chloride ions around the descending limb. This concentration can be as much as four times greater than the normal concentration of tissue fluid.

The walls of the descending limb are permeable to water, and also to sodium and chloride ions. As the fluid flows down this tube, water from it is drawn *out*, by osmosis, into the tissue fluid, because of the high concentration of sodium and chloride ions there. At the same time, sodium and chloride ions diffuse *into* the tube, down their concentration gradient. So, by the time the fluid has reached the very bottom of the hairpin, it contains much less water and many more sodium and chloride ions than it did at the top. The fluid becomes more concentrated towards the bottom of the loop. The longer the loop, the more concentrated it can become.

This concentrated fluid now turns the corner and begins to flow up the ascending limb. Because the fluid inside the loop is so concentrated, it is relatively easy for sodium and chloride ions to leave it and pass into the tissue fluid, even though the concentration in the tissue fluid is also very great. Thus, especially high concentrations of sodium and chloride can be built up in the tissue cells between the two limbs near the bottom of the loop. As the fluid continues up the ascending limb, losing sodium and chloride ions all the time, it becomes gradually less concentrated. However, it is still relatively easy for sodium and chloride to be actively removed, because these higher parts of the ascending loop are next to less concentrated regions of tissue fluid. All the way up, the concentration of sodium and chloride inside the tubule is never very different from the concentration in the tissue fluid, so it is never too difficult to pump sodium and chloride out of the tubule into the tissue fluid.

Thus, having the two limbs of the loop running side by side like this, with the fluid flowing down in one and up in the other, enables the maximum concentration to be built up both inside and outside the tube at the bottom of the loop. This mechanism is called a **countercurrent multiplier**.

But the story is not yet complete! You have seen that the fluid flowing up the ascending limb of the loop of Henle loses sodium and chloride ions as it goes, so becoming more dilute. However, in *Figure 4.9b* you can see that the fluid continues round through the distal convoluted tubule into the **collecting duct**, which runs down into the medulla again. It therefore passes once again through the regions where the concentration of the tissue fluid is very high. Water can therefore be drawn out of the collecting duct, by osmosis, until the concentration of urine is the same as the concentration of the tissue

fluid in the medulla, which may be much greater than the concentration of the blood. The degree to which this happens is controlled by **antidiuretic hormone, ADH,** and is explained in chapter 5.

The longer the loop of Henle, the greater the concentration that can be built up in the medulla, and the greater the concentration of the urine which can be produced. Desert animals such as kangaroo rats, which need to conserve as much water as they possibly can, have especially long loops of Henle. Humans, however, only have long loops of Henle in about one third of their nephrons, the other two thirds hardly dipping into the medulla at all.

Reabsorption in the distal convoluted tubule and collecting duct

The first part of the distal convoluted tubule behaves in the same way as the ascending limb of the loop of Henle. The second part behaves in the same way as the collecting duct, so the functions of this part of the distal convoluted tubule and the collecting duct will be described together.

In the distal convoluted tubule and collecting duct, **sodium ions** are actively pumped from the fluid in the tubule into the tissue fluid from where they pass into the blood. **Potassium ions**, however, are actively transported *into* the tubule. The rate at which these two ions are moved into and out of the fluid in the nephron can be varied, and helps to regulate the amount of these ions in the blood.

SAQ 4.3

a *Figure 4.10* shows the relative rate at which fluid flows through each part of a nephron. If water flows into an impermeable tube, such as a hosepipe, it will flow *out* of the far end at the same rate that it flows *in*. However, this clearly does not happen in a nephron. Consider what happens in each region, and suggest an explanation for the shape of the graph.

b *Figure 4.11* shows the relative concentrations of four substances in each part of a nephron. Explain the shapes of the curves for (i) glucose, (ii) urea, (iii) sodium ions, and (iv) potassium ions.

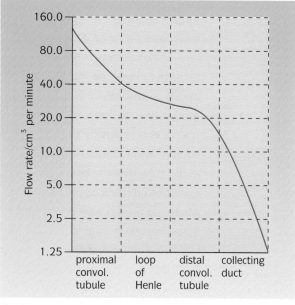

● *Figure 4.10* Flow rates in different parts of a nephron.

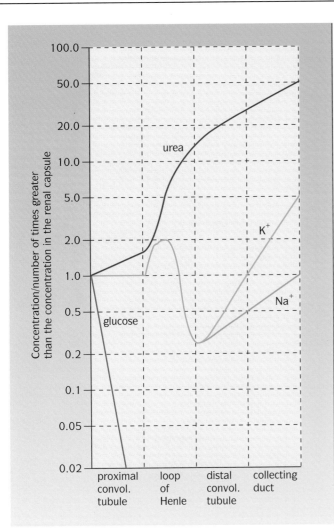

● *Figure 4.11* Relative concentrations of four substances in different parts of a nephron.

Kidney failure and dialysis

Several factors can cause the kidneys to stop working, either temporarily or permanently. This is called **renal failure**. It may be caused by infection, though not necessarily of the kidneys themselves, by damage to the nephrons through poisons such as carbon tetrachloride or mercury, or by damage to the circulatory system resulting in inadequate blood flow to the kidneys. The first signs of renal failure are the retention of salt and water in the body, resulting in **oedema** (swelling of tissues) and a rise in blood pressure. Within a few days, the retention of urea and other excretory substances in the body causes blood pH to drop. If untreated, complete renal failure is fatal within 8–14 days.

People with severe renal failure can be treated by **dialysis**, using an 'artificial kidney'. If the renal failure is caused by poisoning or temporary problems in the circulatory system, dialysis is used until the kidneys heal themselves and begin to work properly again. People suffering from permanent renal failure need regular dialysis or they would die.

The most commonly used method of dialysis is called **haemodialysis**, and uses an artificial kidney machine. *Figure 4.12* shows how this process works. Blood from the patient is taken from a vein, pressurised, and passed through many small channels in the dialyser. Small quantities of heparin are usually added, to stop the blood clotting. The dialyser also contains small channels full of **dialysing fluid**, separated from the blood by a partially permeable membrane, which is usually cellophane. This contains pores that let small molecules, such as water, glucose and urea, and ions, such as Na^+ and Cl^-, diffuse through, but are too small to allow the passage of plasma proteins or blood cells. The high pressure of the blood speeds the removal of urea from the blood, rather like the process of ultrafiltration in the renal capsules of the kidneys.

An alternative method of dialysis uses one of the body's own membranes as the dialysis membrane. The membrane used is the **peritoneum**, which lines the abdominal cavity (*figure 4.14*), and the method is called **peritoneal dialysis**. A tube is inserted into the abdominal cavity under anaesthetic, and left there permanently. Dialysis fluid is passed into the cavity through the tube, and remains there for 24 hours a day, 7 days a week. It is drained out by the patient, and replaced with fresh fluid, three to five times a day. Urea and other excretory substances which have collected in the fluid are therefore removed from the body. Many patients prefer this method to haemodialysis, because they do not have to be 'tied up' to a kidney machine for long periods. They can remain relatively active, moving around freely, and are in control of their own dialysis. Because of this, the process is known as continuous ambulatory peritoneal dialysis, or CAPD. However, there is one disadvantage in that there is a rather greater risk of infection than with haemodialysis.

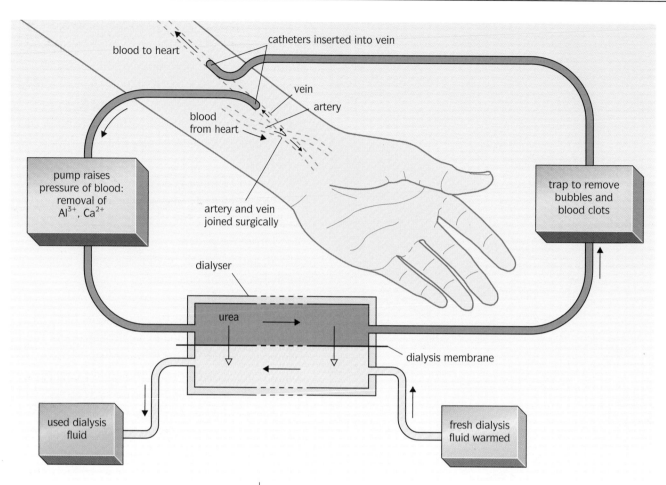

● **Figure 4.12** Haemodialysis.

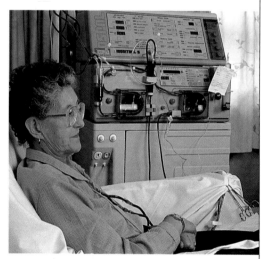

● **Figure 4.13** A patient undergoing renal dialysis.

SAQ 4.4

Table 4.2 shows the relative concentrations of various substances in normal blood plasma, blood plasma from someone suffering from renal failure, and dialysing fluid.

a Which of these substances will be able to diffuse through the dialysis membrane?

b In which direction will each of these substances diffuse?

c Explain why:
  (i) the dialysing fluid contains no urea;
  (ii) the dialysing fluid contains no plasma proteins.

	Relative concentration in		
Substance	normal blood plasma	blood plasma in renal failure	dialysing fluid
glucose	100	100	125
urea	26	200	0
sodium ions	142	142	133
chloride ions	107	107	105
plasma proteins	80	80	0

● **Table 4.2**

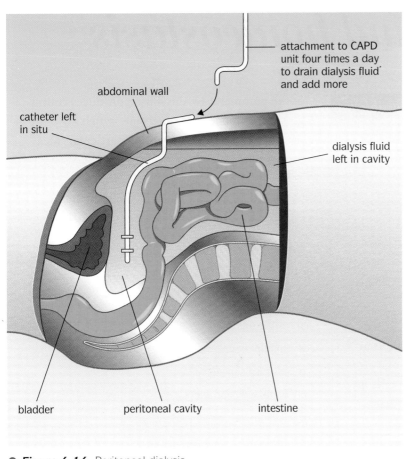

catheter left in situ

abdominal wall

attachment to CAPD unit four times a day to drain dialysis fluid and add more

dialysis fluid left in cavity

bladder   peritoneal cavity   intestine

● *Figure 4.14* Peritoneal dialysis.

Question

1 Discuss the ways in which the structures of different parts of a nephron are adapted to their functions.

2 The table shows information about the relative thickness of the medulla of the kidneys, percentage of the loops of Henle which are long rather than short, and the relative concentration of the urine for three mammals.

Mammal	Relative thickness of medulla	Percentage of long loops of Henle	Relative concentraion of urine
beaver	1.3	0	650
human	3.0	16	1400
desert mouse	10.7	100	5800

Discuss these data.

3 Discuss the roles of active transport in the reabsorption of glucose and water in a kidney nephron.

SUMMARY

■ Toxic waste products of metabolism are removed from the body by the process of excretion. Urea is the main nitrogenous excretory product, formed by the deamination of excess amino acids in the liver. Urea is excreted in solution in water, as urine.

■ The kidneys regulate the concentration of various substances in the body fluids, by excreting appropriate amounts of them. Each kidney is made up of thousands of nephrons and their associated blood vessels. The kidneys produce urine by ultrafiltration and reabsorption, plus some secretion of unwanted substances. Different regions of a nephron have different functions, and this is reflected in the structure of their walls.

■ Blood is brought to the glomerulus in the cup of the renal capsule of the nephron in an afferent arteriole. High hydrostatic pressure in the glomerulus forces substances through the capillary walls, the basement membrane and the wall of the renal capsule into the nephron. The basement membrane acts as a filter, allowing only small molecules through. Most reabsorption occurs in the proximal convoluted tubule, by diffusion and active transport, and also in the distal convoluted tubule and collecting duct. The loop of Henle acts as a countercurrent multiplier, producing high concentrations of salt in the medulla which can draw out water from the collecting duct and produce a concentrated urine.

■ Renal failure can be treated by dialysis.

Chapter five

Control and homeostasis

By the end of this chapter you should be able to:

1 explain what is meant by homeostasis, and outline the principles of negative feedback mechanisms;

2 explain the importance of homeostasis;

3 describe the functioning of the kidney, hypothalamus and pituitary gland in the control of the water content of body fluids;

4 describe the way in which the pH of body fluids is regulated by the respiratory centre in the brain, the kidneys, and by buffers in the blood.

Homeostasis is the maintenance of a stable internal environment within a living organism. In a mammal, the immediate environment of the cells is the tissue fluid which surrounds them. This tissue fluid is derived from blood. In general, homeostatic mechanisms work by controlling the composition of blood, which therefore controls the composition of tissue fluid.

You will probably have dealt already with the way in which blood glucose levels are controlled. The control mechanism for blood glucose levels, like most control mechanisms in living organisms, uses a negative feedback control loop (*figure 5.1*). This involves a **receptor** (**sensor**), a **control** mechanism and an **effector**. The receptor picks up information about the parameter being regulated. This is known as the input. This sets off a series of events culminating in some action by the effector which is called the output. Continuous monitoring

of the parameter by the sensor produces continuous adjustments of the output, which keep the parameter oscillating around a particular 'ideal' level, or set point.

In this chapter, we will look at the way in which two important parameters in the human body are regulated: water content and pH.

SAQ 5.1

Using your knowledge of how enzymes function in metabolism, of respiration, of nervous transmission and of osmosis, explain why changes in any of the following could upset the efficient working of cells:

a temperature;

b glucose concentration;

c water concentration;

d sodium ion concentration;

e pH.

Control of water content

Osmoreceptors, the hypothalamus and ADH

The amount of water in the blood is constantly monitored by cells, called **osmoreceptors**, within the **hypothalamus** (*figure 5.2*). It is not known exactly how these work, but it is probable that differences in water content of the blood cause water to move either into them or out of them by osmosis. When water content of the blood is low, the loss of water from the osmoreceptor cells reduces their volume, which triggers stimulation of nerve cells in the hypothalamus.

These nerve cells are rather different from other nerve cells because they produce a chemical called **antidiuretic hormone**, or **ADH**. ADH is a polypeptide made up of just nine amino acids. It is

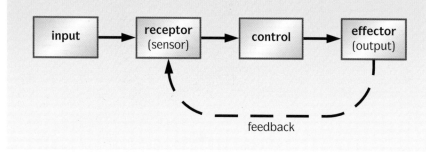

● *Figure 5.1* A feedback loop.

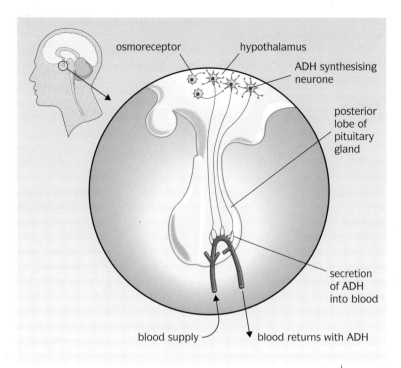

● **Figure 5.2** The secretion of ADH.

made in the cell bodies of the nerve cells, and passes along them to their endings in the **posterior pituitary gland**. When the nerve cells are stimulated by the osmoreceptor cells, action potentials travel down them in the normal way. This causes the ADH to be released from their endings, just as a neurotransmitter would be released. However, ADH does not act as a neurotransmitter. It is secreted into the blood in capillaries in the posterior pituitary gland and is then carried all over the body.

SAQ 5.2

a In what way is the production of ADH *unlike* the production of a neurotransmitter such as acetylcholine?

b In what way is the secretion of ADH *similar* to the release of a neurotransmitter such as acetylcholine?

How ADH affects the kidneys

The target organ for ADH is the kidneys. In particular, ADH acts on the cell surface membranes of the cells making up the walls of the collecting ducts. It makes these membranes more permeable to water than usual (*figure 5.3*).

This change in permeability is brought about by increasing the number of water-permeable channels in the cell surface membrane (*figure 5.4*). The ADH molecule is picked up by a receptor on the cell surface membrane, which then activates an enzyme inside the cell. Inside the cell are ready-made vesicles surrounded by pieces of membrane full of water-permeable channels. The activation of the enzyme by ADH causes these vesicles to move

Low ADH

High ADH

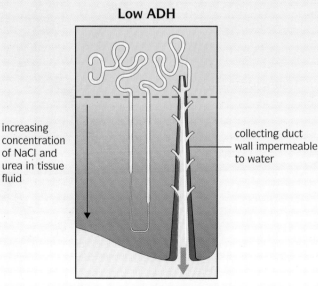

increasing concentration of NaCl and urea in tissue fluid

collecting duct wall impermeable to water

large volumes of dilute urine produced

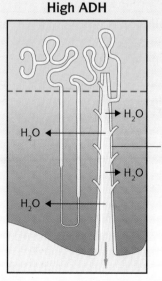

H_2O

H_2O

H_2O

H_2O

collecting duct wall permeable to water allows osmotic absorption of water by the concentrated tissue fluid in the medulla

small volumes of concentrated urine produced

● **Figure 5.3** The effects of ADH on water reabsorption from the collecting duct.

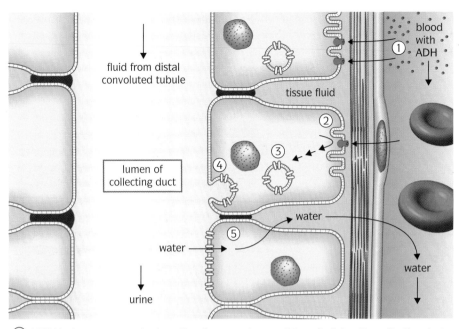

① ADH binds to receptors in the cell surface membrane of the cells lining the collecting duct.

② This activates a series of enzyme-controlled reactions, ending with the production of an active phosphorylase enzyme.

③ The phosphorylase causes vesicles, surrounded by membrane containing water-permeable channels, to move to the cell surface membrane.

④ The vesicles fuse with the cell surface membrane.

⑤ Water can now move freely through the membrane, down its concentration gradient, into the concentrated tissue fluid and blood plasma in the medulla of the kidney.

● *Figure 5.4* How ADH increases water reabsorption in the collecting duct.

Negative feedback in the control of water content

You have seen how the secretion of ADH, brought about as a result of a low blood water content, causes more water to be absorbed back into the blood from the nephrons in the kidney. Thus the maximum amount of water will be retained in the body.

When the blood water content rises, the osmoreceptors are no longer stimulated, and stop stimulating their neighbouring neurones. So ADH secretion stops. This affects the cells in the walls of the collecting ducts. The water-permeable channels are moved out of the cell surface membrane of the collecting duct cells, back into the

to, and fuse with, the cell surface membrane of the cell, so adding many water-permeable channels to it. (If you have learnt how insulin affects the permeability of cells to glucose, you will recognise great similarities between these two mechanisms.)

So, as the fluid flows down through the collecting duct, water is free to move out of the tubule and into the tissue fluid, and it does so because this region of the kidney contains a high concentration of salts. Thus, the fluid in the collecting duct loses water and becomes more concentrated. The secretion of ADH has caused the increased reabsorption of water into the blood. The amount of urine which flows from the kidneys into the bladder will be smaller, and the urine will be more concentrated *(figure 5.5)*.

The word 'diuresis' means the production of dilute urine. Antidiuretic hormone gets its name because it stops dilute urine being produced.

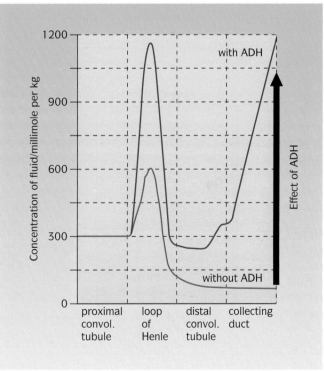

● *Figure 5.5* The concentration of fluid in different regions of a nephron, with and without the presence of ADH.

cytoplasm. Thus, the collecting duct becomes less permeable to water. The liquid flowing down it retains more of its water, flowing into the ureter as a copious, dilute urine.

The collecting duct cells do not respond immediately to the stopping of ADH secretion by the posterior pituitary gland. This is because it takes some time for the ADH already in the blood to be broken down; approximately half of it is destroyed every 15–20 minutes. However, once ADH stops arriving at the collecting duct cells, it takes only 10–15 minutes for the water-permeable channels to be removed from the cell surface membrane and taken back into the cytoplasm for storage.

SAQ 5.3

Construct a flow diagram to show how blood water concentration is controlled. Identify clearly the receptors and effectors, and show how negative feedback is involved.

The role of thirst in regulating water content

As well as causing the production of ADH, the sensing of low blood water content by osmoreceptors in the brain activates **thirst centres** in the brain. This makes you feel thirsty, so you increase the amount of water in your blood by drinking liquids. This mechanism is just as important as the ADH mechanism for controlling the concentration of body fluids.

Drinking water when you are thirsty almost immediately stops the activation of the thirst centres in the brain. This cannot be because the osmoreceptors are no longer being stimulated, as it takes at least half an hour for the water you drink to be fully absorbed and transported around the body. The thirst centres respond directly to the distension of the stomach. Experiments show that inflation of a balloon in the stomach can stop a person feeling thirsty for up to half an hour!

SAQ 5.4

Suggest why it is useful to feel temporary relief from thirst as a result of distension of the stomach.

SAQ 5.5

Add the role of thirst centres to the flow diagram you drew for SAQ 5.3.

Control of pH

pH, acids and bases

pH is a measure of the acidity or alkalinity of a fluid. A pH of 7 is neutral; a pH below 7 is acidic, and a pH above this is alkaline.

A low pH is caused by high concentrations of hydrogen ions, H^+; a high pH is caused by low concentrations of hydrogen ions. An **acid** is a substance which releases hydrogen ions in solution. An acid can be described as **strong** or **weak**, depending on how vigorously it releases hydrogen ions. Thus hydrochloric acid, HCl, is a strong acid, dissociating readily and releasing hydrogen ions freely.

$$HCl \rightarrow H^+ + Cl^-$$

Carbonic acid, H_2CO_3, is a weak acid, as it has only a low tendency to release hydrogen ions.

$$H_2CO_3 \rightleftharpoons H^+ + HCO_3^-$$

A **base** is a substance which combines with hydrogen ions, thus removing them from solution. (Soluble bases are called alkalis, but as 'base' is the more general term, we will use it here. Do not confuse it with the 'bases' in DNA!) As for acids, bases can be strong or weak depending on their tendency to do this. The hydrogencarbonate ion, HCO_3^-, is a weak base that combines with hydrogen ions to form carbonic acid.

$$H^+ + HCO_3^- \rightleftharpoons H_2CO_3$$

Haemoglobin is also a base. As you have seen in chapter 1, it combines with hydrogen ions to form haemoglobinic acid.

The importance of controlling pH

The pH of human body fluids is normally around 7.4 in arterial blood, and 7.35 in venous blood and tissue fluid. It is important that this pH be kept constant, as even small changes in pH can greatly affect protein structure and damage the workings of cell membrane proteins and intracellular and extracellular enzymes. The lowest limit at which anyone can survive for more than a few hours is a pH of about 6.8, while the upper limit is a pH of 8.

SAQ 5.6

Suggest why the pH of arterial blood is higher than the pH of venous blood and tissue fluid.

There are several ways in which the body regulates pH. These are:

■ by means of **buffers**;
■ by the **respiratory centre** in the brain;
■ by the **kidneys**.

pH control by buffers

A buffer is a substance which can absorb or release hydrogen ions depending on their concentration in a solution. If hydrogen ion concentration is high, producing a low pH, the buffer absorbs hydrogen ions. If hydrogen ion concentration is low, producing a high pH, the buffer releases hydrogen ions.

In the human body, **buffer systems** are very important in the control of pH. The most important of these is the **hydrogencarbonate buffer system**.

Carbonic acid is produced in the body when carbon dioxide is released by respiring cells and reacts with water. As you have seen, carbonic acid is a weak acid; that is it has only a weak tendency to dissociate into hydrogen ions and hydrogencarbonate ions.

$$H_2CO_3 \rightleftharpoons H^+ + HCO_3^-$$

All weak acids act as buffers. If carbonic acid is in a solution which contains a high concentration of hydrogen ions (low pH), its tendency to dissociate is even lower than usual and the balance of the equation shifts to the left. If the carbonic acid is in a solution which contains a low concentration of hydrogen ions (high pH), the balance of the equation shifts to the right.

Thus, the carbonic acid–hydrogencarbonate system acts as a buffer. In a low pH, it produces fewer hydrogen ions, so raising the pH. In a high pH, it produces more hydrogen ions, so lowering the pH.

Many **proteins** also act as buffers. **Haemoglobin** is one of these, and the way in which it acts as a buffer is described on page 17. Proteins behave as buffers because some of their amino acids contain groups which can either accept or release hydrogen ions. These groups include the amino group at one end of the polypeptide chain and the carboxyl group at the other, plus R groups on certain amino acids such as glutamate, lysine and cysteine, which themselves contain amino or carboxyl groups.

pH control by the respiratory centre

You have seen that carbon dioxide from respiration produces carbonic acid which weakly dissociates to produce hydrogen ions. High carbon dioxide concentrations therefore reduce the pH of the blood.

Within the medulla oblongata of the brain is an area known as the **respiratory centre** (*figure 5.6*). The respiratory centre controls the rate at which the intercostal muscles and diaphragm contract and relax to produce breathing movements. The basic rhythm of breathing is produced by regular, repetitive action potentials from this part of the brain. These action potentials are transmitted along nerves to the muscles which bring about breathing.

The respiratory centre contains receptors that are sensitive to the hydrogen ion concentration. However, these receptors are separated from the blood by the relatively impermeable blood–brain barrier (page 6) across which hydrogen ions cannot pass. So the receptors cannot respond to the hydrogen ion concentration of the blood. However, carbon dioxide can cross the blood–brain barrier without difficulty. It dissolves in the tissue fluid to form carbonic acid which dissociates to produce hydrogen ions. The receptors can respond to these ions to bring about an increase in the rate of breathing (*figure 5.6*).

If the amount of carbon dioxide in the blood is high, then the respiratory centre sends impulses to the breathing muscles which increase the rate and depth of breathing (*figures 5.7 and 5.8*). This results in a larger volume of air moving more quickly into and out of the alveoli, and so increases the rate at which carbon dioxide is removed from

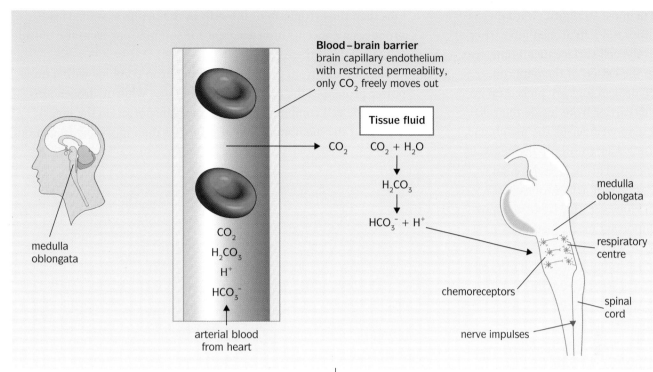

● *Figure 5.6* How high blood carbon dioxide levels increase the rate of breathing.

the blood. As the blood concentration of carbon dioxide drops, the pH consequently rises back towards normal. These changes occur so quickly that the amount of carbon dioxide in the blood hardly varies, even during strenuous exercise.

SAQ 5.7

Describe and explain the shapes of the curves in *figure 5.7* and *figure 5.8*.

pH control by the kidneys

The kidneys are able to regulate pH by altering the rate at which they excrete hydrogen ions and hydrogencarbonate ions. When blood pH is low they excrete an acidic urine. When blood pH is high they excrete a basic (alkaline) urine.

Secretion of hydrogen ions

Hydrogen ions can be secreted into the fluid in most parts of the nephron, by the cells in the nephron walls. The more hydrogen ions that are secreted into the fluid, the more will be excreted in the urine which is produced from it. Two different mechanisms of hydrogen ion secretion are used *(figure 5.9)*.

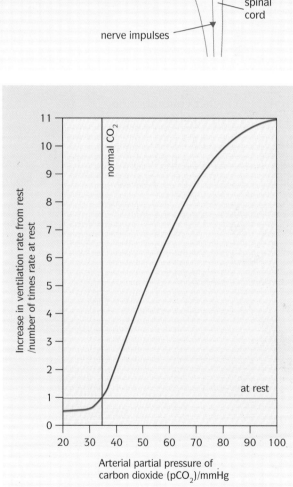

● *Figure 5.7* The effect of arterial carbon dioxide concentration on ventilation rate. **Ventilation rate** is the amount of air entering and leaving the lungs per unit time. Breathing faster, breathing more deeply, or both, will increase the ventilation rate.

The most straightforward mechanism uses a hydrogen ion carrier in the cell surface membrane next to the lumen of the nephron. Hydrogen ions are picked up by this carrier from inside the cell and moved across the membrane, using ATP to supply the necessary energy. This is, therefore, an example of active transport.

However, this is not the most important mechanism for hydrogen secretion. In most parts of the tubule, hydrogen ion secretion is associated with the movement of sodium ions in the opposite direction.

The basal membranes of cells lining the nephron have a sodium–potassium pump, which produces a higher concentration of sodium ions outside the cell than inside it. This results in the fluid in the nephron having a higher concentration of sodium ions than the cytoplasm of the cells in the nephron wall. This produces a concentration gradient for sodium ions from the outside to the inside of these cells.

Sodium ions from the fluid in the nephron combine with a transporter protein in the cell surface membrane, while hydrogen ions within the cell combine with the same transporter on the inner surface of the membrane. The transporter then moves hydrogen out

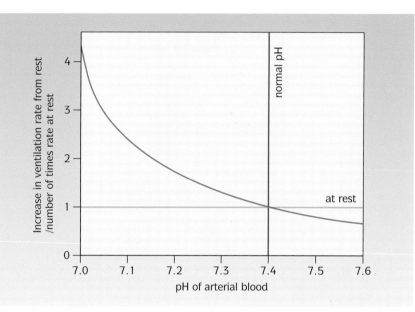

● **Figure 5.8** The effect of the pH of arterial blood on ventilation rate.

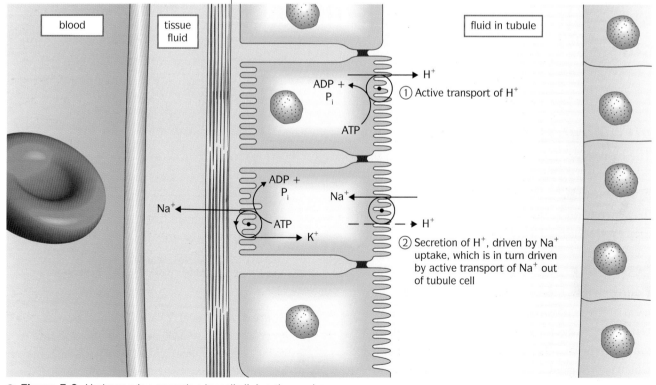

● **Figure 5.9** Hydrogen ion secretion by cells lining the nephron.

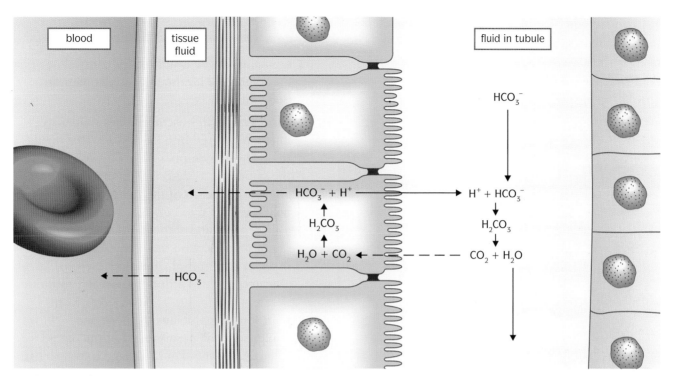

● *Figure 5.10* Reabsorption of hydrogencarbonate ions by cells lining the nephron.

and sodium in, simultaneously. ATP is not needed for this, because the sodium ions are moving down their concentration gradient, which supplies enough energy to move the hydrogen ions against their concentration gradient. However, ATP *is* needed to fuel the sodium–potassium pump which produced the sodium ion gradient in the first place.

The rate at which hydrogen ions are secreted into the fluid in the nephron depends on the concentration of hydrogen ions, or pH, in the blood. A low blood pH results in a high rate of hydrogen ion secretion, while a high blood pH results in a low rate.

Reabsorption of hydrogencarbonate ions

Hydrogencarbonate ions are continually being filtered out of the blood into the renal capsule. As they pass along the nephron, they join the hydrogen ions which have been secreted into the fluid. They react with them, to form carbonic acid, which then dissociates into carbon dioxide and water (*figure 5.10*). The carbon dioxide diffuses into the tubule cells, while the water remains in the fluid in the tubule, eventually being excreted in the urine.

Within the tubule cell, this carbon dioxide, together with other carbon dioxide formed by respiration in the cell itself or brought to it in the blood, may react with water under the influence of the enzyme carbonic anhydrase. This forms carbonic acid, which then dissociates to form hydrogencarbonate ions and hydrogen ions. You have already seen that the hydrogen ions are secreted into the fluid in the tubule. The hydrogen-carbonate ions diffuse out of the cell in the other direction, not into the fluid in the tubule but into the tissue fluid around the cell and from there into the blood.

Thus, by a rather roundabout mechanism involving several changes of identity along the way, hydrogencarbonate ions are removed from the tubule and reabsorbed into the blood.

How can this help to regulate the pH of the blood? If blood pH is low, that is there are too many hydrogen ions and not enough hydrocar-bonate ions, then when they meet each other in the fluid in the kidney tubules some of the hydrogen ions will not have a hydrogencarbonate ion to combine with. These left-over hydrogen ions combine with buffers in the urine and are excreted.

If, on the other hand, blood pH is too high, then it will be hydrogencarbonate ions which are 'left over' in the kidney tubule. These will remain in the fluid and be excreted in the urine.

SUMMARY

■ The water content of the blood is controlled by changing the amount of water excreted in the urine. This is done by regulating the permeability of the walls of the collecting ducts to water, and hence the amount of water reabsorbed from the collecting ducts into the blood. The permeability is altered by the hormone ADH, which is secreted by the posterior pituitary gland in response to stimulation of osmoreceptors in the hypothalamus.

■ The pH of body fluids is regulated by buffers, the respiratory centre and the kidneys. Buffers, especially the hydrogencarbonate buffer system and proteins, mop up excess hydrogen ions in body fluids and release them if there are not enough in solution. The respiratory centre responds to high carbon dioxide concentration, which produces a low pH, by stimulating faster and deeper breathing. This increases the rate of removal of carbon dioxide from the blood. The kidneys can vary the rate at which they secrete hydrogen ions and reabsorb hydrogencarbonate ions; any imbalance in these results in a more acidic or more alkaline urine being excreted, bringing a low or high blood pH back towards normal.

Question

1 Compare the mechanisms for controlling blood glucose levels and water content in body fluids.

2 Most vertebrates use hormones similar to mammalian ADH, to help with water regulation. These hormones do not always work in the same way as described in this chapter. Suggest how each of the following might help the animal to conserve water.

   a In reptiles and amphibians the hormones not only increase the permeability of the distal tubules and collecting ducts to water, but also reduce glomerular filtration rate.

   b In some amphibians the hormone increases the permeability of the outer surface of the skin to sodium ions.

   c In toads the hormone increases the permeability of the walls of the urinary bladder to water.

3 People who climb to high altitudes, where the air is thin, may suffer from mountain sickness if they do not breathe extra oxygen.

   a Suggest how the low concentrations of oxygen at altitude may affect each of the following:
      (i) the functioning of brain cells;
      (ii) the rate of functioning of the sodium–potassium pump, and therefore the functioning of the kidneys.

   b The low concentrations of oxygen stimulate faster breathing, so that the concentration of carbon dioxide in the blood becomes low. Suggest and explain the effects this may have on each of the following:
      (i) the pH of the blood;
      (ii) the pH of the urine.

Chapter six

The liver

By the end of this chapter you should be able to:

1   describe the gross structure of the liver including its blood supply;

2   describe the structure of a liver lobule;

3   explain the functions of the liver in carbohydrate metabolism, fat metabolism, storage of vitamins A, B and D, production of bile, synthesis of plasma proteins, breakdown of haemoglobin, deamination and detoxification.

The liver is one of the largest organs in the body. It lies just beneath the diaphragm *(figure 6.1)*, towards the right-hand side of the body, and is made up of several lobes. It is supplied with blood by two blood vessels. The **hepatic artery** leads from the aorta and delivers oxygenated blood to the

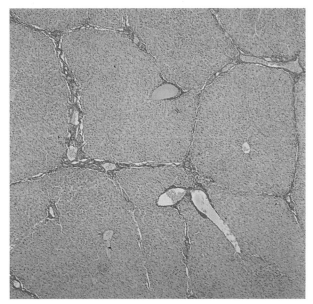

● *Figure 6.2* Light micrograph of a section of liver tissue. In the centre of each lobule there is a branch of the hepatic vein. In the 'corners', between the lobules, are branches of the hepatic artery, hepatic portal vein and bile duct.

liver. The **hepatic portal vein** leads from the small intestine and delivers blood rich in absorbed nutrients. One vessel, the **hepatic vein**, carries blood away from the liver to the vena cava.

The liver contains many **lobules**; there are up to 100 000 in a human *(figures 6.2 and 6.3)*. In the centre of each lobule is a branch of the hepatic vein. Between the lobules are branches of the hepatic artery and hepatic portal vein. Blood flows from these, through the lobule, and into the branch of the hepatic vein.

The lobules are made up of many liver cells, or **hepatocytes**, arranged in rows, radiating out from the centre like spokes in a wheel. The channels which carry the blood between these rows of cells are called **sinusoids**. Other channels carry a fluid called **bile** which is secreted by the liver. These channels are called **bile**

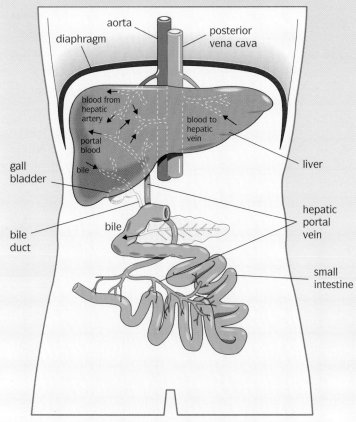

● *Figure 6.1* The structure of the liver and its associated organs.

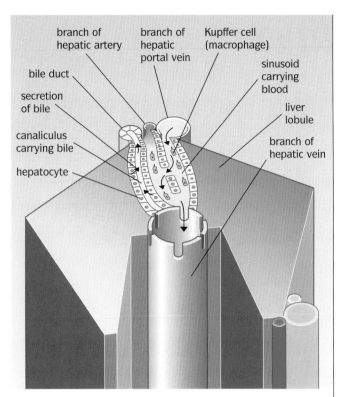

● **Figure 6.3** The structure of a liver lobule.

canaliculi. The bile flows from the centre of the lobule towards the outside, where it enters a branch of the **bile duct.**

The liver has a very large number of functions, some of which have already been described in earlier chapters. These will be mentioned again briefly here, and other functions described in more detail. The functions include:

■ carbohydrate metabolism,
■ fat metabolism,
■ bile formation,
■ storage of vitamins,
■ synthesis of plasma proteins,
■ breakdown of haemoglobin,
■ detoxification,
■ deamination of amino acids.

Carbohydrate metabolism

The liver is involved in the control of blood glucose levels, in conjunction with the hormones insulin, glucagon and adrenaline. When blood glucose levels are high, β cells in the islets of Langerhans in the pancreas secrete insulin. This causes the liver to take up glucose from the blood at a faster rate than usual, thus reducing blood glucose levels. Some of the glucose taken up is converted to the storage poly-saccharide **glycogen.** When blood glucose levels are low, α cells in the islets secrete glucagon, which stimulates the breakdown of glycogen to glucose in the liver. This is described in more detail in *Foundation Biology* in this series.

The liver can also produce glucose from amino acids, glycerol or lactate, in a process known as **gluconeogenesis** ('making new glucose'). These substances are first converted to **pyruvate** and then, through a

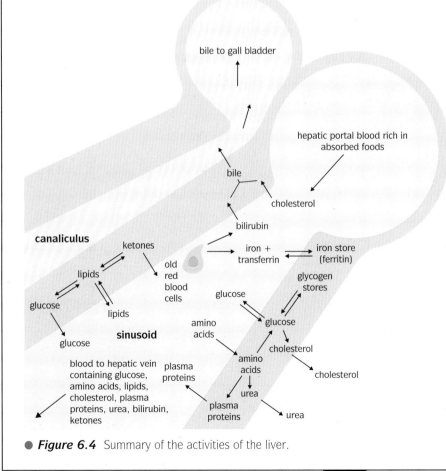

● **Figure 6.4** Summary of the activities of the liver.

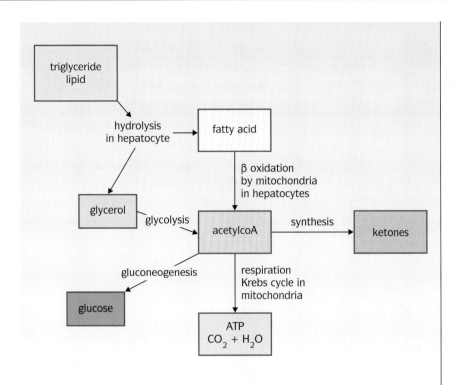

● *Figure 6.5* Summary of lipid metabolism.

Fat metabolism

Fats as an energy source

Fats can be used in respiration to provide energy. They are an important energy source at all times. Cardiac muscle uses fatty acids as its preferred respiratory substrate. If no carbohydrates have been eaten during a period of up to a day, or exercise levels are high so that carbohydrate stores are used up, then fats are increasingly used by other body tissues also.

The liver can use fat as a respiratory substrate. Fat molecules inside cells are first split into fatty acids and glycerol. The fatty acids are then split and combined with coenzyme A to form acetyl-coenzyme A which can be fed into the Krebs cycle to produce ATP (*figure 6.5*).

Some of the fatty acids are converted into ketones in the liver. These are taken in the blood to other parts of the body where cells can use them as a respiratory substrate.

series of steps, to glucose. The process can be thought of as 'glycolysis in reverse', although this is not absolutely true as several of the steps and enzymes involved are not common to both processes.

Gluconeogenesis has a very important role in keeping cells supplied with enough glucose. Brain cells, in particular, require a constant supply of glucose for respiration; for example a typical adult human brain needs about 120 g glucose per day. Glycogen reserves are only enough to provide one day's supply, so if you do not eat enough carbohydrate in any one day, it is essential to produce glucose from non-carbohydrate sources.

Synthesis of triglycerides

The liver is also responsible for much of the conversion of excess carbohydrate and protein to fat (*figure 6.6*). Some of this fat is **triglyceride**. Once made, the triglyceride is transported in the blood to other parts of the body where it is stored in adipose tissue.

As fats are insoluble in water, they cannot be transported just as they are. Triglycerides are combined with protein molecules to form lipoproteins. Most triglycerides are transported as **very**

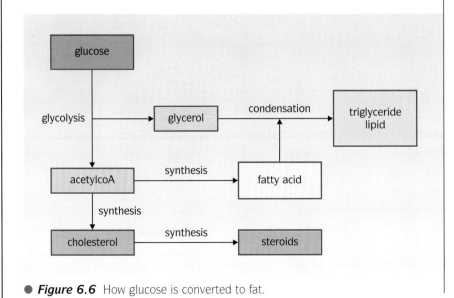

● *Figure 6.6* How glucose is converted to fat.

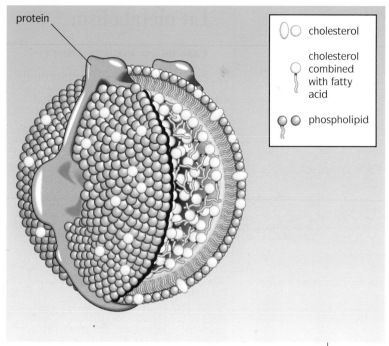

cholesterol

cholesterol combined with fatty acid

phospholipid

protein

● **Figure 6.7** A low density lipoprotein (LDL).

low density lipoproteins *(figure 6.7)*. A lipoprotein is a particle made up of many lipid and protein molecules. The centre is filled with hydrophobic lipids, while the outside consists of a 'shell' of polar lipids and proteins. There are many types of lipoproteins which carry different types of fats from and to different parts of the body. They are named according to their relative density.

Synthesis of cholesterol

The liver makes **cholesterol**. Cholesterol is not a lipid, but it is lipid soluble and can be combined with fatty acids to form lipids.

Cholesterol is present in the diet, especially in meat, eggs and dairy products. Although cholesterol is frequently reported to be bad for you, it is important to realise that it is an essential component of the body, and that the harm it does may well have been overstated. It is an important component of cell membranes. It is also needed for the synthesis of steroid hormones, such as oestrogen and testosterone. Cholesterol is deposited in the skin, which it helps to waterproof, so preventing both loss of water by evaporation from the body and uptake of water-soluble substances from outside. Vitamin D is made from cholesterol, in skin cells stimulated by

ultraviolet light. Cholesterol is also used for making bile salts (page 68.)

Cholesterol is not water-soluble, and so is transported in the blood plasma in combination with proteins, as lipoproteins. Some cholesterol is transported as very low and low density lipoproteins, along with triglycerides, and some as **high density lipoproteins**.

The relative proportion of low density and high density lipoproteins in the blood appears to affect the risk of developing **atherosclerosis**. Atherosclerosis, or 'hardening of the arteries', occurs when cholesterol is deposited on the inner walls of blood vessels, forming plaques which stiffen the walls and narrow the space through which blood can flow *(figure 6.8)*. Low density lipoproteins in the blood tend to be associated with the deposition of cholesterol as plaques, whereas high density lipoproteins may protect against this, or even be able to remove it. Thus a high ratio of high density to low density lipoproteins can reduce the risk of atherosclerosis and heart attack. However, the evidence for these effects is not clear, and they probably vary considerably in different people. A person's genotype may have more influence on the likelihood of suffering from coronary heart disease than does diet.

When cholesterol is eaten and absorbed from the small intestine, the liver responds by decreasing

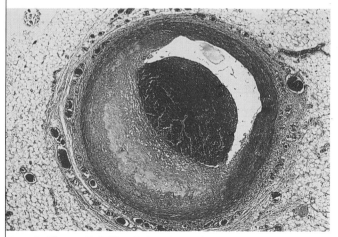

● **Figure 6.8** The dark red area in the centre of this artery is a blood clot. Its formation was triggered by the plaque which has developed in the wall, narrowing the lumen.

the rate at which it synthesises cholesterol. This is because the dietary cholesterol reduces the activity of one of the enzymes which catalyses the synthesis of cholesterol from acetylcoenzyme A. Thus, dietary cholesterol does not always have a significant effect on the amount of cholesterol in the blood. However, this effect varies greatly from one person to another. On the other hand, large quantities of saturated fats in the diet cause the liver to increase the rate at which it converts these to cholesterol. So, if you are watching your diet to try to keep down blood cholesterol level, it is more important to reduce the amount of saturated fats you eat than to reduce the amount of cholesterol you eat.

Production of bile

Most of the cholesterol formed in the liver is used to make bile. In a human, about $1000\,\text{cm}^3$ of bile are made each day. Bile is made by the hepatocytes and secreted into the bile canaliculi. These carry some of the bile into the **bile duct** and then into the duodenum. Some is carried into the **gall bladder**, where it is stored and concentrated before being released into the bile duct.

Apart from water, the major component of bile is **bile salts**. These are made from cholesterol. When secreted into the duodenum, they act as detergents and emulsify fats, so that the fats can be more easily digested by lipase, and more easily absorbed into the lacteals in the villi. Bile salts are recycled. About 94% of them are reabsorbed into the blood in the villi, to be taken up by the liver and reused to form bile.

Bile also contains cholesterol. Exactly what its function is in bile is not known; it may just be there as a by-product of bile salt production. Normally, this cholesterol interacts with the bile salts to form water-soluble particles, but sometimes (for example, if there is too much cholesterol in the bile, or too little water or bile salts) it may precipitate out and form gallstones (*figure 6.9*). Sometimes, gallstones may contain calcium deposits as well as cholesterol. The gallstones may remain in the gall bladder, or get into the bile duct and block it. They can be very painful and may prevent bile from flowing into the duodenum, so interfering with digestion of fats. Gallstones can be removed by surgery, or by ultrasound treatment which breaks them into many tiny pieces so that they flow away in the bile. Gallstones containing only cholesterol can be dissolved away by giving the patient extra bile acids over a period of a few years.

Bile also contains breakdown products from red blood cells. This is described on pages 72–3.

Storage of vitamins

The liver stores the fat-soluble vitamins **A** and **D**, and also the water-soluble vitamin $\mathbf{B}_{12}$. Enough of these vitamins are usually held in the liver to last for up to a year, assuming that none are eaten in the diet.

Vitamin A is **retinol**. It is needed for the formation of retinal, which is part of the light-absorbing pigment found in rod cells in the retina of the eye. It is also important for the synthesis of glycoproteins which help to keep epithelial tissues moist, for growth, normal bone formation and the process of repair of epithelial tissues. Vitamin A deficiency prevents the shedding

● *Figure 6.9* These gallstones were removed from the gall bladder on the left.

and repair of these surface cells, so that epithelia become thick and dry. The cornea of the eye become opaque, and often becomes infected, causing blindness. This is a common cause of blindness in developing countries.

We get vitamin A from foods of animal origin, such as dairy products. It is added artificially to margarine. The orange plant pigment, carotene, can be converted in the body to retinol, so carrots and other vegetables are also indirect sources of this vitamin.

Vitamin A is carried from the liver to tissues all over the body in the blood plasma, attached to a protein. The synthesis of this protein is very dependent on the intake of protein in the diet, so a person suffering from a deficiency of protein in the diet may also suffer from symptoms of vitamin deficiency, even if their intake of vitamin A is quite high.

Vitamin D is **calciferol**. It is needed for the formation of a hormone 1,2,5-dihydroxy cholecalciferol (calcitriol), which controls the metabolism of calcium and phosphorus, and their absorption into the blood from foods in the alimentary canal. The formation of this hormone from calciferol takes place in the liver. A shortage of vitamin D leads to the disease rickets, where not enough calcium is laid down in bones, so that they fail to harden properly. A child with rickets has soft, bendy bones, and the leg bones become bowed.

Most of our vitamin D is obtained from the action of sunlight, especially ultraviolet wavelengths, on cholesterol in the skin. It is also found in fish oils, dairy products and eggs, and is artificially added to some margarines.

Vitamin B_{12} is **cobalamin**. It is a very complex molecule, containing an atom of the element cobalt. It is needed for the production of a coenzyme called coenzyme B_{12}, whose roles in the human body are still being discovered. A deficiency of vitamin B_{12} causes the disease pernicious anaemia, in which the number of red blood cells gradually declines, leading to death if not treated. This deficiency is normally caused not directly by a lack of B_{12} in the diet, but by a lack of a compound called **intrinsic factor,** which is normally made by the stomach wall and which helps vitamin B_{12} to be absorbed across the wall of the ileum into the blood. It is treated by giving monthly injections of the vitamin.

Vitamin B_{12} is unusual in that the only organisms which can make it are microorganisms. Neither plants nor animals can make it. However, it is found in all foods of animal origin, so most people do not suffer from a shortage of it in their diets. Plant products contain no vitamin B_{12}, so vegans may need to take vitamin B_{12} supplements which are produced commercially from microorganisms.

Synthesis of plasma proteins

The blood contains many different kinds of proteins dissolved in the plasma. These are called **plasma proteins**. They include fibrinogen, globulin and albumin. Almost all of the plasma proteins, except for antibodies, are made in the liver.

Fibrinogen and **prothrombin** are important in blood clotting (page 13).

Globulin is a term used for most of the globular proteins in blood plasma. Some of these are γ (gamma) globulins, that is antibodies. These are *not* made by the liver but by cells of the immune system. The other globulins are made by the liver. Many of them help to transport other molecules, such as thyroxine, insulin and lipids, by combining with them in the blood plasma.

Albumin is the same protein as that found in egg white. There is more albumin than any other plasma protein in human blood. Its main function is to form a colloid in blood plasma. The albumin molecules are too large to escape from capillaries into tissue fluid, and so keep the osmotic concentration of the blood high enough to stop too much water leaving the blood (pages 7–8). Like globulins, albumin also helps in the transport of substances such as steroid hormones, bilirubin and mineral ions.

Breakdown of haemoglobin

Red blood cells have a life span of about 120 days. After this, they become fragile and are broken down. Much of this breakdown occurs in the spleen, which is a very soft organ lying just below the diaphragm on the left side of the body near the stomach. The breakdown of old red blood cells releases haemoglobin from them, which goes into solution in the blood plasma. This haemoglobin is taken up by phagocytic cells in many parts of the body, including lymph glands, the spleen and the liver. The phagocytic cells in the liver are called **Kupffer cells.**

Inside the phagocytic cells, the iron is removed from the haemoglobin molecules and then combined with a plasma protein called transferrin *(figure 6.10).* The transferrin–iron complex is released back into the blood, from where it may be taken up by cells in the bone marrow and used for making new haemoglobin. Alternatively, it may be taken up by hepatocytes and changed into a molecule called ferritin and stored to be used when required.

The remainder of the haemoglobin molecule, from which iron has been removed, is converted in the phagocytic cells into a greenish-yellow compound called **bilirubin**. If the bilirubin has been formed in phagocytic cells not in the liver, then it is released into the blood plasma where it combines with albumin and is transported around the body. On arrival at the liver, it is taken up by the hepatocytes and secreted into bile. It is bilirubin which gives bile its greenish colour. Bilirubin is an excretory product; it has no function in bile, but is simply on its way out of the body.

If a person has too much bilirubin circulating in their blood, they look yellowish and are said to have jaundice. This can be a result of gallstones; if the bile cannot flow into the duodenum, then bilirubin cannot be excreted and builds up in the blood plasma. Newborn babies often have slight jaundice, especially if they are premature, because their hepatocytes may not yet have developed sufficiently to be able to take up bilirubin and excrete it in bile. The breakdown of bilirubin is helped by ultraviolet light, and this is often used to reduce jaundice in newborn babies.

Deamination of amino acids

This is described on pages 46–7.

Detoxification

As blood passes through the liver, many drugs, such as alcohol and antibiotics, are taken up by the hepatocytes and broken down. This often occurs on the smooth endoplasmic reticulum in the hepatocytes.

In a similar way, steroid hormones such as oestrogen and testosterone are broken down in the liver. If the liver is badly damaged, for example as a result of cirrhosis of the liver, these hormones may build up in concentration in the blood. Males with liver cirrhosis may begin to show feminine features, while females may begin to show male features, as a result of the build-up of these steroid hormones.

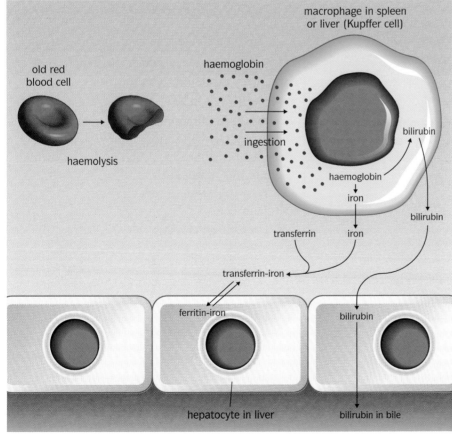

● *Figure 6.10* The fate of haemoglobin from old red blood cells.

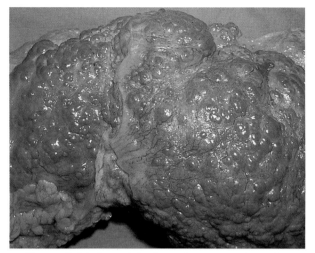

● *Figure 6.11* Part of the liver of a person who suffered from liver cirrhosis, as a result of drinking large quantities of alcohol over a long period.

Cirrhosis of the liver *(figure 6.11)* is the development of fibrous tissue inside it which destroys the liver cells and constricts the blood vessels. Cirrhosis may be caused by the ingestion of poisons such as carbon tetrachloride or by virus diseases such as hepatitis. However, the commonest cause of cirrhosis is alcoholism, in which the ingestion of large quantites of alcohol over long periods of time causes irreversible damage to the liver.

SUMMARY

■ The liver is a very large and metabolically active organ, which plays many important roles.

■ It helps in homeostasis by interacting with the pancreas in the regulation of blood glucose levels.

■ It is involved in the use of fats as an energy source, and in making triglycerides and cholesterol.

■ It stores vitamins A, D and B_{12}, and iron in the form of ferritin.

■ The liver makes bile, which contains bile salts to emulsify fats in the duodenum, and the bile pigment bilirubin. Bilirubin is an excretory product which is formed from the breakdown of haemoglobin.

■ The liver makes plasma proteins, such as fibrinogen, globulins and albumin.

■ It deaminates excess amino acids, producing urea for excretion by the kidneys.

■ It detoxifies drugs and breaks down hormones.

Questions

1 Discuss the role of the liver in homeostasis.

2 Discuss the ways in which the structure of the liver is related to its functions.

3 Hepatitis is a disease of the liver, caused by pathogenic (disease-causing) viruses which damage liver cells. Suggest how damage to the liver may produce each of the following symptoms of hepatitis.
   a Poor digestion of fats
   b Jaundice
   c Poor blood clotting

Answers to self-assessment questions

Chapter 1

1.1 a Size is important, but is not the only factor. Microscopic organisms such as *Paramecium* do not have transport systems, whereas all large organisms such as green plants, fish and mammals do. However, cnidarians do not have transport systems even though some of them are considerably larger than insects, which do.

b Level of activity is important. Animals such as fish and mammals have a transport system containing a pump; plants, most of which are less active than most animals, do not have a pump. Insects have pumps in their transport system, even though they are smaller than the less active cnidarians, which do not have a pump.

1.2 a The fish has a single circulatory system, whereas the mammal has a double circulatory system. In the fish, blood leaves the heart and travels to the gills, where it picks up oxygen, before continuing around the body. In the mammal, the blood returns to the heart after picking up oxygen at the lungs, and is then pumped around the body.

b Oxygenated blood can be pumped around the body at a higher pressure, and therefore faster, in a mammal than in a fish, because pressure is lost in the capillaries in the gills. This can provide a more efficient oxygen supply to mammalian cells than to fish cells.

c Endothermy requires large amounts of oxygen, as heat is released by respiration in which glucose (or other metabolites) is combined with oxygen in cells. Thus endothermic animals must have an efficient oxygen supply to their cells. Fish cells may need less oxygen, as it is not required for heat production.

1.3 a Elastic fibres allow the artery to stretch and recoil as blood pulses through. Nearer the heart, the pressure changes between systole and diastole will be greater, and the maximum systolic pressure greater, than anywhere else in the circulatory system. Thus more elastic fibres are needed to cope with these large pressures and pressure changes.

b If arteries cannot expand as a surge of blood at high pressure enters them, they are more likely to burst. Moreover, the build-up of cholesterol narrows the lumen, so forcing blood through a narrower space, which can increase its pressure, further increasing the risk of the blood vessel bursting. There is also a risk of the vessel becoming permanently blocked.

1.4 Blood cells, and haemoglobin in red blood cells, would cause scattering and absorption of light before it reached the retina. The aqueous humour supplies the cornea with its requirements.

1.5 a Gravity pulls blood downwards. Normally, contraction and relaxation of leg muscles squeezes in on leg veins; valves in them ensure blood moves upwards and not downwards. When standing to attention, these muscles are still, so blood accumulates in the feet.

b As thoracic volume increases, pressure inside the thorax decreases. This decreases the pressure in the blood vessels in the thorax. The effect is very small in the arteries, but more significant in the veins. The relatively low pressure of the blood in the veins in the thorax, compared with the pressure in veins elsewhere in the body, produces a pressure difference causing blood movement towards the thorax.

1.6 Answers to this may be found in the text.

1.7 Answers should include reference to: the fluctuating pressure in arteries; why the fluctuations become gradually less as the blood passes through the arterial system; the rapid drop in pressure as the blood flows along the arterioles and capillaries and reasons for this; the rise of pressure as blood enters the pulmonary circulation via the right-hand side of the heart, but not so high as the pressure in the aorta, and reasons for this.

1.8 a The larger the relative molecular mass, the lower the permeability.

b Net diffusion for glucose would be into the muscle. Respiration within the muscle requires glucose, so that its concentration within the muscle cells is lower than in the blood plasma.

c Albumin in the blood plasma raises its solute concentration (osmotic pressure), thus helping to draw water back from the tissue fluid into capillaries. If albumin could diffuse out of capillaries into tissue fluid, more water would accumulate in the tissue fluid. (This is called oedema.)

1.9 a Protein in tissue fluid comes from the cells making up the tissues, many of which secrete proteins.

b If plasma protein concentrations are low, then, as explained in SAQ 1.8c above, water will not be drawn back into capillaries from tissue fluid.

1.10 2.1×10^{11}

1.11 a Anaerobic respiration – yes; this occurs in the cytoplasm, and red blood cells have all the necessary enzymes.

b Aerobic respiration – no; this occurs in mitochondria which red blood cells do not have.

c Protein synthesis – no; there is no DNA, so no mRNA can be transcribed.

d Cell division – no; there are no chromosomes, so mitosis cannot occur, nor are there centrioles for spindle formation.

e Lipid synthesis – no; this occurs on the smooth endoplasmic reticulum, and there is none.

f Active transport – yes; this occurs across the cell surface membrane, and can be fuelled by ATP produced by anaerobic respiration.

1.12 a $195\,cm^3$

b $25\,cm^3$

1.13 a (i) 96.5%
(ii) $1.25\,cm^3$

b (i) 24.0%
(ii) $0.31\,cm^3$

Chapter 2

2.1 a (i) 0.7–0.8 seconds
(ii) 60/0.8 = 75 beats per minute
For **b**, **c**, **d**, **e** and **f**, see figure below.

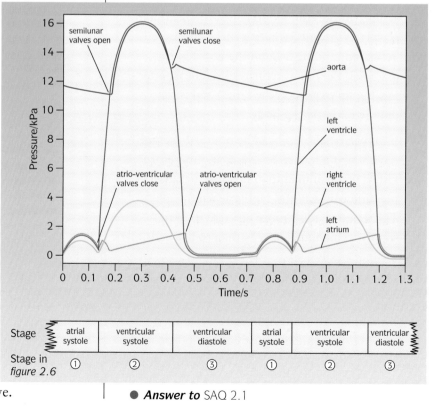

● **Answer to** SAQ 2.1

2.2 **a** 1 beat = about 20 mm on the grid.

25 mm on the grid represents 1 second.

So 20 mm represents $\frac{20}{25}$ seconds = 0.8 seconds.

If one beat lasts 0.8 seconds, then in 1 second there are $\frac{1}{0.8}$ beats.

So in 1 minute there are $\frac{1 \times 60}{0.8}$ = 75 beats.

b (i) This is the time during which the ventricles are contracting.

(ii) On the grid, the distance betweeen Q and T is about 7 mm.

This represents $\frac{7}{25}$ = 0.28 seconds.

c (i) This is the time when the ventricles are relaxed, and are filling with blood.

(ii) On the grid, the distance between T and Q is about 13 mm.

This represents $\frac{13}{25}$ = 0.52 seconds.

A quicker way of working this out is to subtract your answer to b(ii) from 0.8 seconds.

d (i) By performing varying levels of exercise.

(ii) See figure.

(iii) As heart rate increases, contraction time remains constant, but filling time decreases. This indicates that the increase in heart rate is produced by a shorter time interval between ventricular contractions, rather than by a faster ventricular contraction.

The more frequent contractions increase the rate of circulation of blood around the body, providing extra oxygen to exercising muscles. If this was done by shortening the time over which the ventricles contract, much of the advantage would be lost, as less blood would probably be forced out by each contraction. By shortening the time *between* contractions, the amount of blood pumped out of the heart per unit time is increased.

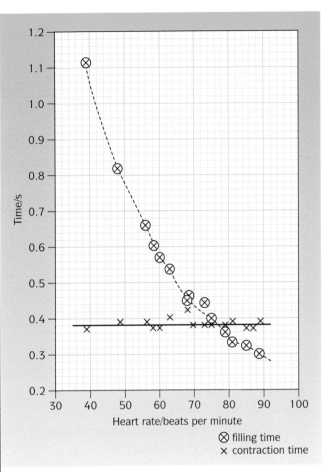

● **Answer to** SAQ 2.3d(ii)

Chapter 3

3.1 **a** Increased wind speed moves water vapour away from the leaf more rapidly, thus maintaining a steeper water potential gradient between the air spaces of the leaf and the surrounding air.

b Rise in temperature increases the kinetic energy of water molecules which move, and therefore diffuse, more rapidly. High temperatures may also decrease the humidity of the air (as warm air can hold more water), so increasing the diffusion gradient.

3.2 Mammals use the evaporation of water in sweat for cooling purposes; the water evaporates from the skin surface, absorbing heat energy. Thus the two processes are very similar.

3.3 a In plants, osmosis is involved in the uptake of water from soil into the root hair. It may also be involved in movement from cell to cell across the root, but only if the water moves through the cell surface membranes of the cells. If it travels by the apoplast pathway, or via plasmodesmata between cells, then osmosis is not involved. Movement across the root endodermis does involve crossing cell surface membranes, so osmosis is again involved here. In the leaf, osmosis is involved if water moves into the cytoplasm of a cell across the cell surface membrane, but not if it moves by the apoplast pathway or plasmodesmata, as in the root.

In animals, osmosis is involved in the movement of water from the ileum and colon into the cells lining these parts of the alimentary canal, and then out of these cells into the blood. The water again moves by osmosis when leaving the blood and entering cells in body tissues. Osmosis is also involved in the reabsorption of water from nephrons.

b In plants, mass flow is involved in the movement of water up the xylem vessels.

In animals, mass flow is involved in the movement of blood plasma (containing water) along the blood vessels.

3.4 a The total lack of cell contents provides an uninterrupted pathway for the flow of water.

b Lack of end walls also provides an uninterrupted pathway for the flow of water.

c The wider the diameter, the more water can be moved up through a xylem vessel per unit time. However, if the vessels are too wide, there is an increased tendency for the water column to break. The diameter of xylem vessels is a compromise between these two requirements.

d The lignified walls provide support, preventing the vessels from collapsing inwards.

e Pits in the walls of the vessels allow water to move into and out of them.

3.5 Sucrose, amino acids, ATP and plant growth substances.

3.6 Sources: storage tissue of a potato tuber when the buds are beginning to sprout.

Sinks: nectary, developing fruit, developing potato tuber.

3.7 All the required contents of this comparison table are in the text on pages 34–42. Care should be taken that equivalent points are kept opposite each other.

Chapter 4

4.1 a From the glomerulus.

b Proteins.

c It will increase the solute concentration of the blood plasma, increasing the osmotic gradient between the filtrate and the blood.

4.2 A large percentage (60%) of the water in the fluid is reabsorbed in the proximal convoluted tubule; thus the amount of water in which the urea is dissolved decreases. This increases the concentration of urea in the fluid.

4.3 a Flow rate is highest at the beginning of the proximal convoluted tubule, where fluid is entering via filtration into the renal capsule. As the fluid flows along the proximal convoluted tubule, a large percentage of it is reabsorbed, thus decreasing its volume. There is thus less fluid to flow, so less passes a given point in unit time: in other words, its flow rate decreases.

This reabsorption continues all along the nephron, which is why the flow rate continues to drop. The rate of flow decreases rapidly in the collecting duct, as a high proportion of water may be reabsorbed here.

b (i) Glucose concentration drops rapidly to zero as the fluid passes through the proximal convoluted tubule, because all of it is reabsorbed into the blood at this stage.
(ii) Urea concentration increases because water is reabsorbed from the tubule.

(iii) The concentration of sodium ions remains constant in the proximal convoluted tubule, as, although some sodium is reabsorbed here, this is balanced out by the reabsorption of water. In the loop of Henle, the countercurrent multiplier builds up sodium ion concentration in the lower parts of the loop; the concentration drops as you pass up the ascending limb towards the distal convoluted tubule, as sodium ions are lost from the tubule. In the distal convoluted tubule, sodium ions are actively pumped out of the tubule, so you might expect their concentration to drop. However, this is counterbalanced by the continued removal of water from the tubule, which results in an increasing concentration.

(iv) As for sodium ions, until the distal convoluted tubule, where potassium ions are actively transported into the tubule, so increasing their concentration more than that of sodium.

4.4 **a** Glucose, urea, sodium and chloride ions.

b Glucose diffuses from dialysing fluid into the blood.
Urea, sodium and chloride diffuse from blood into dialysing fluid.

c (i) To maximise the diffusion gradient, so maximising the rate at which urea is removed from the blood.
(ii) There is no need for plasma proteins: there would be no function which they would serve. It does not matter that there are not any, because they are unable to pass through the membrane, and so will not be lost from the blood.

Chapter 5

5.1 **a** Low temperatures reduce kinetic energy of molecules, thus reducing reaction rates; so they would slow metabolism. High temperatures increase the likelihood of denaturation of proteins, thus causing damage to structures

such as cell membranes which contain proteins, and also slowing and stopping enzyme-controlled reactions.

b Glucose is needed as a fuel by body cells. Low glucose concentrations result in the use of other substances as a respiratory substrate, which can produce acidic waste products (see *Foundation Biology* page 72). This can damage cells. High glucose concentrations may cause osmotic problems (see **c**).

c High or low water concentrations of body fluids can cause water to move into or out of cells by osmosis. Large increases or decreases in the amount of water in a cell may cause structural damage (for example bursting or shrinkage), and affect many metabolic reactions, as water is needed as a solvent for reagents and may also be a reagent itself.

d Sodium ion concentration indirectly affects water concentration, and so may result in the problems described in **c** above. High sodium ion concentrations may cause the retention of larger amounts of water in the body fluids (by osmotic effects) and so cause increased blood pressure. Changes in sodium ion concentration may affect the sodium–potassium pump (see *Foundation Biology*).

e pH changes affect proteins. Excessively high or low pH can break ionic and hydrogen bonds that hold proteins in shape. This can cause structural damage to cells. Most importantly, pH changes affect the action of enzymes which can normally only function efficiently within a narrow pH range.

5.2 **a** ADH is not made and stored near the presynaptic membrane of a neurone. It is made in the cell body and transported along the axon of the neurone.

b ADH, like neurotransmitters, is released from the neurone when an action potential arrives.

5.3 There are many possible ways in which this flow diagram could be constructed. It should show the following:
input (change in blood water concentration) to sensor (osmoreceptor cells); resulting in secretion of ADH from posterior pituitary if water concentration low; producing output (change in rate of water reabsorption) by effector (walls of collecting duct); and negative feedback to sensor.

5.4 As there is a time delay between drinking the water and its absorption and transfer around the body, the osmoreceptors will not be aware that water has been drunk until half an hour or so afterwards. If you continued feeling thirsty until the osmoreceptors responded to the increase in water content of the blood, you would carry on drinking and would end up with far too much water in the blood. By responding to the distension of the stomach, this long time delay is much reduced, so reducing the amount of oscillation in the water control system.

5.5 The way in which the thirst centres are incorporated will vary according to the original design of the flow diagram.

5.6 Arterial blood (apart from that in the pulmonary artery) will contain less carbon dioxide than venous blood (apart from that in the pulmonary vein). Carbon dioxide reacts with water to produce carbonic acid which is a weak acid and so lowers pH.

5.7 a *Figure 5.7* shows how ventilation rate changes with carbon dioxide concentration in the blood.

At rest, when the carbon dioxide concentration is about 35 mm Hg, ventilation rate is taken to be 1. If carbon dioxide concentrations drop below this, ventilation rate drops a little, but not significantly. However, if carbon dioxide concentrations rise above this level, then ventilation rate rises in response. The relationship is almost linear up to carbon dioxide concentrations of around 80–5 mm Hg, becoming less steep above this value.

The increase in ventilation rate is brought about by the respiratory centre in the medulla oblongata. Carbon dioxide from the blood combines with water and then dissociates, forming hydrogen ions which stimulate receptors in the respiratory centre. These stimulate the production of action potentials at a faster rate, which are transmitted along nerves to the intercostal muscles and the muscles of the diaphragm. These contract faster and harder, so increasing both rate and depth of breathing, and hence the ventilation rate.

b *Figure 5.8* shows how ventilation rate changes with pH of arterial blood. pH is a measure of hydrogen ion concentration. A low pH indicates a high hydrogen ion concentration.

The curve shows that ventilation rate decreases with increasing pH, the greatest rate of change occurring at lower pHs.

Blood is normally slightly alkaline. The presence of carbon dioxide lowers pH, because carbon dioxide reacts with water to produce hydrogen ions. Thus, the explanation for the shape of this curve is similar to that for *figure 5.7*. It appears to be the other way round because a *low* pH represents a *high* carbon dioxide concentration.

This curve only shows information for a pH range from 7.0 upwards. The maximum ventilation rate is just over four times normal, which is equivalent to that given by a carbon dioxide concentration of around 50 mm Hg on *figure 5.7*.

Index (Numbers in italics refer to figures.)